The Early Elementary Grammar Toolkit

T0383568

Teaching grammar can be overwhelming and is often an overlooked part of effective instruction, especially for young learners. *The Early Elementary Grammar Toolkit* to the rescue! This comprehensive guide makes grammar instruction in the K–2 classroom fun and meaningful.

You will learn how to:

◆ Teach grammar in a practical and applicable way by presenting each grammar rule as a useful writing tool for students.
◆ Use mentor texts—excerpts from great literature—to help students understand grammar in action.
◆ Promote metacognition along the way so that students become responsible for their own learning.
◆ Implement innovative instructional strategies and tools aligned with national and state standards.

Throughout the book, you'll find step-by-step recommendations for teaching grammatical concepts to young learners, including the use of punctuation, capitalization, parts of speech, and more. With standards-based resources and activities for grades K–2, the book includes tips addressing teaching for each of these grades, classroom snapshots that show you the tools in action, flowcharts, infographics, and specific instructional recommendations to engage students.

Sean Ruday is an associate professor of English education at Longwood University and a former classroom teacher. He frequently writes and presents on innovative ways to improve students' literacy learning. You can follow him on Twitter at @SeanRuday and visit his website at www.seanruday.weebly.com.

Kasey Haddock is a kindergarten teacher in Virginia. She has a true passion for shaping and molding the minds of future generations and laying the early foundations of students' education. You can follow her on Twitter at @haddock_kasey.

The Early Elementary Grammar Toolkit

Using Mentor Texts to Teach Grammar and Writing in Grades K-2

Sean Ruday and Kasey Haddock

Routledge
Taylor & Francis Group

NEW YORK AND LONDON

Cover image: © Getty Images

First published 2023
by Routledge
605 Third Avenue, New York, NY 10158

and by Routledge
4 Park Square, Milton Park, Abingdon, Oxon, OX14 4RN

Routledge is an imprint of the Taylor & Francis Group, an informa business

© 2023 Taylor & Francis

The right of Sean Ruday and Kasey Haddock to be identified as authors of this work has been asserted in accordance with sections 77 and 78 of the Copyright, Designs and Patents Act 1988.

ISBN: 978-1-032-29818-4 (hbk)
ISBN: 978-1-032-28517-7 (pbk)
ISBN: 978-1-003-30220-9 (ebk)

DOI: 10.4324/9781003302209

Typeset in Palatino
by Apex CoVantage, LLC

Access the Support Material: www.routledge.com/9781032285177

"The meaning of life is to find your gift. The purpose of life is to give it away."—William Shakespeare

This book is in memory of my sweet Momma, Tammy Bray Haddock. She found her gift of caring and advocating for others and spent 40 years of her life dedicated to her nursing career. Much of who I am and what I have learned in life resembles her service to others. I am blessed to share that same passion and lead a life of purpose through my teaching career.

~ Kasey Haddock

Contents

Meet the Authors

Sean Ruday is Associate Professor and Program Coordinator of English Education at Longwood University and a former classroom teacher. He began his teaching career at a public school in Brooklyn, New York, and has taught English and language arts at public and private schools in New York, Massachusetts, and Virginia. Sean frequently writes and presents on innovative ways to improve students' literacy learning. You can follow Sean on Twitter at @SeanRuday and visit his website at www.seanruday.weebly.com.

Kasey Haddock is a graduate of Longwood University. She grew up in Virginia Beach, where she currently teaches kindergarten. Kasey has a true passion for shaping and molding the minds of future generations and laying the early foundations of students' education. She has a love for children's literature and believes in the power of reading aloud and the importance of exposing children to books at an early age. You can follow Kasey on Twitter at @haddock_kasey.

Acknowledgments

Sean's Acknowledgments

I want to thank everyone at Routledge Eye on Education—especially amazing editor Karen Adler—for the insight, guidance, and support.

I would like to thank my parents, Bob and Joyce Ruday. I am grateful for their encouragement in all aspects of my life.

Finally, I want to thank my wife, Clare Ruday. I can't imagine my life without the happiness she brings to it.

Kasey's Acknowledgments

First and foremost, I want to thank my former professor, Dr. Ruday. Thank you for believing in me and giving me the opportunity to collaborate with you on this project.

I would like to thank my parents, Leland and Tammy Haddock. I am grateful for such strong role models who shaped me into the person I am today. I would not be where I am without your love and support.

I would like to thank my second grade teacher, Jeri Blythe, who inspired me to be a teacher. I grew up wanting to graduate from Longwood University and become a teacher. I am truly living my dream!

Finally, I want to thank all of my former and future students, for when you learn, I learn. Your curiosity, excitement, and love for learning continue to keep my passion alive.

Support Material

Many of the tools, reproducible charts, forms, and infographics in this book are also freely available on the Routledge website as downloadable Support Material. The specific tools from Appendix B and infographics available online are listed in what follows. You can access these downloads by visiting www.routledge.com/9781032285177. Then click on the tab that says, "Support Material" and select the files. They will begin downloading to your computer.

List of Tools

Introduction

Using Mentor Texts to Unlock the Tools of Grammar and Writing With Young Learners

Writing in the early elementary years is a very developmental process (Barone et al., 2005). When students are in kindergarten, the focus in the beginning of the year is teaching alphabet knowledge. Once students have mastered letter recognition and letter sound knowledge, they are ready to begin applying that knowledge into writing. Students begin writing by simply drawing pictures and orally dictating their writing. Students then move toward using beginning sounds to label their pictures. Students are eventually able to sound out words to write one or more sentences. As students make progress in their writing, you work to "fine-tune" their writing by reminding them to put a capital letter at the beginning of the sentence and a period at the end of the sentence. As students move on to first and second grades, they are introduced to more grammatical concepts. There is often no explanation for the importance of these concepts other than what they are and don't forget to include them.

Instruction in the early elementary years is centered around literature. Read alouds are shared to reinforce math concepts, introduce reading concepts, and explain science and social studies concepts. Books are often used during writing instruction for students to generate ideas and write about experiences. Books can also be used as mentor texts to introduce and teach different grammatical concepts: students are able to see concrete examples of potentially abstract concepts. It puts meaning to concepts that students may not know the importance of and also helps them recognize and better understand concepts that they might be using in their writing and not even realize it. In this book, we discuss how early elementary teachers can use mentor texts and intentional grammar instruction to equip their students with the tools of effective writing.

The Power of Mentor Texts

In a recent professional development workshop on grammar instruction that Sean conducted, he was asked about programs, websites, and software marketed to help improve students' understanding of and ability to use grammar.

DOI: 10.4324/9781003302209-1

In response to the question, Sean took a step back and looked at the many outstanding children's books that lined the walls of the elementary school classroom in which the workshop was being held. Motioning to these books, Sean explained, "The best program for grammar instruction is around us right now. All of these amazing books that engage our students also represent the most effective way to teach our students about grammar and writing." He continued to elaborate on why published books represent such an effective way to help students learn grammar: "Through these works, our students are able to see authentic, real-world examples of grammatical concepts that make writing as effective as possible. They're able to see the moves writers make and why they make them. Also, very importantly, they're able to see grammatical concepts as tools for effective writing, not just things they do that are out-of-context and disconnected from writing."

We believe that the term "mentor texts" is a very powerful one: to us, in the context of grammar instruction, it means a work that exemplifies how experts use grammar and writing strategies to maximize the effectiveness of their works. In other words, grammar-focused mentor texts are models of excellent writing that we can use to teach our students. When we show our students engaging and accessible examples of grammatical concepts that we want them to understand and eventually use in their writing, we're providing them with meaningful models that can inform their own uses of that concept. For example, if we're working with our students on the grammatical concept of conjunctions, we can use a model of how a published author uses that concept to maximize the effectiveness of their work. One such exemplar of conjunction use is found in the first sentence of Ezra Jack Keats' (1962) classic *The Snowy Day*, which reads "One winter morning Peter woke up and looked out the window" (n.p.). In this sentence, Keats uses the conjunction "and" to maximize the sense of flow in the work. If he did not make use of this conjunction, the information would be choppier and have less continuity; it might read "One winter morning Peter woke up. He looked out the window." While this new version wouldn't be incorrect, it also wouldn't be as clearly written and as easy to read as the original text. When talking with our students about grammatical concepts such as conjunctions, we can use mentor texts to make them accessible, to provide concrete and authentic examples of their use, and to show why they are important to effective writing.

The National Council of Teachers of English (2016), in its position statement "Professional Knowledge for the Teaching of Writing," asserts that "In order to provide high-quality writing opportunities for all students, teachers need to understand how writers read for the purposes of writing—with an eye toward not just what the text says but also how it is put together" (para.

6). This insight is particularly important to the mentor-text-based approach to grammar and writing instruction described in this book: when we connect reading and writing in our classrooms, we provide our students with authentic opportunities to see how published authors use important grammar and writing tools in their works. By doing so, we help our students look at grammatical concepts in meaningful and authentic ways. The use of mentor texts in grammar instruction provides students with opportunities to thoughtfully consider the choices that writers make, the reasons for those choices, and how they can ultimately apply that same thought process to their own works. It helps our students read as writers in the ways the National Council of Teachers of English describes.

A Tool-Based Approach to Teaching Grammar and Writing

As we use mentor texts to help students understand essential aspects of effective grammar and writing, we create a situation in which our students can see the grammatical concepts that writers use as tools that maximize the effectiveness of their works. As the use of the word "Toolkit" in this book's title suggests, the idea of tools is essential to the instructional approach we discuss in this book. The method of grammar instruction that we'll share with you in these pages is designed to help students think of grammatical concepts as tools that are strategically and purposefully incorporated into writing at appropriate times. For example, just as we would use a hammer in a specific situation and a screwdriver in another one, writers use the elements of grammar when they are in situations that align with the uses of those elements. The excerpt in the preceding section from Keats' (1962) *The Snowy Day* provides an excellent example of this purposeful use: the conjunction "and" is incorporated strategically in order to maximize the flow and continuity of the statement. Keats' decision to use this grammatical concept is based on the situation and is the best grammar tool to fit the context.

Another excellent example of a purposefully implemented grammatical concept is the use of verbs in the 2016 book *Last Stop on Market Street*, written by Matt de la Peña and illustrated by Christian Robinson. For instance, the excerpt "From the bus stop, he watched water pool on flower petals. Watched rain patter against the windshield of a nearby car" (n.p) is an outstanding representation of how vivid and strong verbs look in writing and the impact they can have on a piece. The verbs "watched," "pool," and "patter" clearly convey the actions described in the text. If the author had instead used more general and less descriptive verbs, readers wouldn't be able to understand the events of the story as well. For example, the verb "patter" in the statement

"Watched rain patter against the windshield of a nearby car" tells readers exactly how the rain landed on the car windshield. If de la Peña had written "Watched rain land against the windshield of a nearby car," we would not understand the action with as much clarity and specificity. As these examples illustrate, the grammatical concept of strong and vivid verb use is a key writing tool that Matt de la Peña uses to maximize the effectiveness of *Last Stop on Market Street*.

When we think about grammatical concepts as tools for effective writing, we move toward a new way of considering grammar instruction in general. Instead of regarding grammar and grammar instruction as isolated from writing instruction and based primarily on worksheet use and out-of-context explanations, this tool-oriented approach views grammatical concepts as tactics that authors purposefully and strategically use to make their writing better. By approaching grammar and writing instruction in this way, we can help our students gain an awareness of the impact of specific grammatical concepts on the effectiveness of writing. This awareness is a form of metacognition, which is knowledge of a cognitive phenomenon (Flavell, 1979) and is often thought of as thinking about thinking (Garner, 1987). Although metacognition in general has been around for a long time, it has only recently been applied to thinking about grammar (Ruday, 2013, 2020a). When applied directly to grammar instruction, metacognitive thinking involves teachers and students discussing topics such as why a writer chose to use a certain grammatical concept and the effect that concept had on a particular piece of writing. For instance, the discussions of conjunction use in *The Snowy Day* (Keats, 1962) and strong and vivid verbs in *Last Stop on Market Street* (de la Peña & Robinson, 2016) shared so far in this chapter illustrate what a tool-oriented approach that emphasizes metacognitive awareness of grammatical concepts can address.

The Importance of This Approach to Early Elementary Grammar and Writing Instruction

While mentor-text-based and metacognition-oriented approaches to grammar and writing instruction are currently utilized in grades from upper elementary through high school (Ruday, 2017, 2020a, 2020b), we believe this instructional method can also be transformative in the early elementary period of kindergarten, first grade, and second grade. As students begin to engage with written texts in these grades and take steps toward understanding what writing is and what it looks like, we feel they are perfectly suited to begin to think about the tools of grammar, language, and writing in age-appropriate, supportive, and engaging ways. By showing our early elementary students relevant and grade-level-aligned examples of published mentor texts, we can help them develop strong foundations in the tools of writing and grammar, building their abilities to think about what those tools are and why writers use them.

The connection between mentor texts and one's own writing that we describe in this book can be powerful and impactful: students see what published authors do, consider the importance of the tools they use, and begin to apply those ideas to their own works. What better time to begin to engage students in this process than when they are beginning their journeys as writers? While there are many aspects of effective writing instruction (Graham, 2019), there are two that we believe are essential to the growth of early elementary school students and to the principles discussed in this book: 1) reading and writing are related, and 2) all students are writers (NCTE, 2016). By emphasizing the connection between reading and writing and helping students see those ideas as related, we can build their awareness of the moves that authors make and the purposeful ways they use grammatical concepts and other writing strategies in their own works. When we convey to students that they are all writers, we construct a classroom environment in which they all are encouraged to think about how they'll apply what they noticed in the mentor texts they read to their own writing. We feel that these two ideas are especially relevant to the writing development of early elementary students to help them build a strong sense of writing self-efficacy at early ages. This self-efficacy can help students continue to see themselves as writers as they continue through their schooling careers and their lives.

For instance, while engaging with the book *Where The Wild Things Are* (Sendak, 1963), students could look closely at the grammatical concepts author Maurice Sendak uses to make this story particularly effective. One example of an exemplary use of grammatical concepts in *Where The Wild Things Are* is the line "'And now,' cried Max, 'let the wild rumpus start'" (n.p.). In this excerpt, Sendak uses a strong and vivid verb ("cried"), a clear and descriptive adjective ("wild"), and a specific noun that helps the reader understand what's taking place "rumpus." When reading or listening to this text, students can think about these grammatical concepts and the impacts they have on us as an audience, such as the way these tools of language help us develop a clear and detailed awareness of what is taking place. By developing our students' awareness of the purposeful ways authors like Maurice Sendak use grammatical concepts and the impact they have on the piece, we can help those students think differently about grammar and see it as a set of tools for effective writing. This way of thinking about and considering grammatical concepts will help our students build their understanding of those concepts and ultimately apply them to the pieces of writing that they create. As students engage in this mentor-text-based process, they can see the close connections between the pieces they read and the writing that they do. In addition, as our students put these tools of grammar and writing into action, they can all see themselves as writers who employ similar strategies to those used by published authors.

What to Expect in This Book

This book is designed to be a resource for early elementary school (kindergarten, first grade, and second grade) teachers who are interested in rethinking grammar instruction. Specifically, the book describes a mentor-text-based and metacognition-oriented approach to teaching grammar that has the power to both engage students and to help them think about the impact that purposefully used grammatical concepts have on writing. Before we (Kasey and Sean) began writing this book, we identified ten key grammatical concepts that we feel are very important for early elementary school students to understand and are also addressed in relevant state and national language and writing standards for kindergarten, first, and second grades. Those concepts, as well as the chapters in which they appear, are identified in the table that follows.

Grammatical Concept	Chapter
Understanding and Using Nouns	1
Understanding and Using Verbs	2
Creating Complete Sentences	3
Using End Punctuation	4
Using Capitalization	5
Using Question Words	6
Implementing Conjunctions	7
Indicating Plurals	8
Using Commas	9
Using Pronouns	10

Figure 0.1 Grammatical Concepts and Chapters

In each of these ten chapters, we'll discuss what the focal grammatical concept is, why it is important to effective writing in the early elementary classroom, and how teachers can help their students understand these concepts and implement them in their writing. The ideas, mentor text examples, and instructional practices described in these chapters are designed to guide teachers as they talk with their students about what key grammatical concepts are, why they are important to effective writing, and how they can use them as they continue to grow as writers and communicators. For consistency and ease of use, Chapters 1 through 10 are divided into the following sections:

◆ An overview of the fundamental features of the chapter's focal concept.
◆ A discussion of why the concept is important to good writing, including examples of how published authors use the concept in their own works.
◆ A "Classroom Snapshot" that describes how Kasey taught her kindergarten students about the chapter's focal concept. This section provides concrete examples of what the instructional approach discussed in this book can look like in action.
◆ Some specific instructional recommendations for teachers to use when teaching the concept to their own students.
◆ A flowchart that visually represents the instructional recommendations described in that chapter.
◆ A one-page infographic that illustrates key components of the instructional processes discussed in the chapter.
◆ An infographic that depicts examples of published mentor texts that represent effective use of the chapter's focal concept.

In addition to these chapters that describe specific suggestions for teaching grammatical concepts aligned with the early elementary grades, this book also features additional resources that will help you put the ideas discussed in this text into action. Chapter 11 provides ideas for assessing students' knowledge of grammatical concepts in student-centered and meaningful ways and the book's concluding chapter contains final thoughts and tips for classroom practice designed to guide you as you apply the insights discussed in this book. This book also features an annotated bibliography, which contains the following information: 1) the titles, authors, and illustrators of the texts that we discuss in this book as exemplars of particular grammatical concepts, 2) a key grammatical concept found in each work, 3) an excerpt from that work, found earlier in this book, that demonstrates exactly how the author uses that grammar concept, and 4) information on the chapter of this book in which the concept is discussed (in case you want to refer back to the text for more information on a concept). The annotated bibliography is designed to make this book as user-friendly as possible. It is organized alphabetically by author's last name and each entry includes important details designed to help you use mentor texts to teach these grammatical concepts. Finally, this book includes reproducible charts and forms that you can use in your classroom: another resource we've included to maximize the usefulness and applicability of this book.

By taking a mentor-text-based approach to early elementary school grammar instruction that helps students see grammatical concepts as tools for effective writing, we can provide our students with authentic and meaningful experiences with grammar and writing that will continue to serve them well in their academic careers and in their lives. The ideas and details we share in this book will provide you with the information you need to put this instructional approach into action. So, if you're ready to begin the journey to innovative and engaging early elementary school grammar instruction, keep reading!

1 🔧

Building Blocks

The Importance of Nouns to Effective Writing

What Are Nouns?

In this chapter, we'll begin our exploration of grammatical concepts and their importance to effective writing by thinking about an essential tool that writers use to communicate information and construct sentences: the concept of nouns. Nouns are often referred to as naming words: they are words used to refer to people, places, things, or ideas. When we're writing and we want to name something, we use a noun. For example, a writer might say "The fans filled the stadium" when describing a sporting event. In this sentence, the nouns "fans" and "stadium" are used to identify important components of the situation: "fans" identifies the people in the sentence, while "stadium" names the thing they filled. Figure 1.1 provides key information about nouns: it defines what they are and provides examples of each of the noun categories.

It's important to note that nouns can be either common or proper: common nouns refer to general people, places, things, or ideas, while proper nouns refer to specific examples. In Figure 1.1, the first two nouns in each category of people, places, things, and ideas are common nouns, while the second two in the category are proper nouns. For instance, in the category of places, "town" and "school" are common nouns because they refer to general places instead of specific ones. Conversely, the places "New York City" and "Atlantic Ocean" are proper nouns because they name particular locations. Since proper nouns identify specific examples, they are capitalized, while common nouns, because they refer to general concepts, are not—unless they begin a sentence. (We'll discuss

DOI: 10.4324/9781003302209-2

What are nouns?	Nouns are words used to refer to people, places, things, or ideas.
What are examples of nouns that refer to people?	friends, teacher, LeBron James, Taylor Swift
What are examples of nouns that refer to places?	town, school, New York City, Atlantic Ocean
What are examples of nouns that refer to things?	planet, computer, Google, Facebook
What are examples of nouns that refer to ideas?	freedom, belief, Impressionism, Hinduism

Figure 1.1 Key Noun Information

Common Nouns	Possible Corresponding Proper Nouns
building	Empire State Building
store	Target
shoes	Air Jordans
television show	*Sesame Street*
singer	Demi Lovato
stadium	Wrigley Field
city	Los Angeles
holiday	Halloween

Figure 1.2 Common Noun and Possible Corresponding Proper Nouns

these capitalization-related concepts even further in Chapter 5, which specifically focuses on capitalization.) Figure 1.2 provides more information on this topic; it lists common nouns and proper nouns that can correspond with them.

Why Nouns Are Important to Effective Writing

Nouns are essential tools for effective writing: authors use nouns in their works to convey to their readers the people, places, things, and ideas they are discussing. By using nouns effectively, writers help their readers understand exactly what is being talked about in a passage. To maximize the effectiveness of noun use, authors often use the most clear and specific nouns they can. This doesn't mean that authors always use proper nouns, but instead refers to how writers frequently choose words that allow readers to understand a person, place, thing, or idea in a clear, specific, and easy-to-understand way. For example, if a writer uses the noun "building" in a sentence, readers will have some idea of what is being described. However, if a writer uses a more specific and clear noun such as "skyscraper," readers will gain a much stronger understanding of the noun in the sentence.

Published authors use clear and specific nouns to maximize the effectiveness of their works. For example, in the book *Under the Mango Tree* (Mark & Cloud, 2021), author Valdene Mark uses specific nouns to help readers understand the features of the tree that is central to the book. In the sentence "Vee and Sanaa loved playing under the mango tree, its branches wide and tall, its bough heavy and strong" (Mark & Cloud, 2021, n.p.), the author not only names the specific type of tree under which Vee and Sanaa play, but also clearly and concretely identifies aspects of the tree that are particularly noteworthy. By using the specific nouns "branches" and "bough," Valdene Mark helps readers understand exactly what aspects of the tree have these characteristics. If the author instead used a vague and general term such as "parts," readers would not be able to determine the specific features of the tree being described. The specific nouns "branches" and "bough" help readers develop a clear understanding of the tree and ensure that those readers can visualize it in the way the author intended.

Another outstanding example of clear and effective noun use is found in the book *Freedom Soup* (Charles & Alcántara, 2021), which describes a Haitian grandmother and granddaughter's experiences making a traditional soup while talking about Haitian history and culture. When describing the music playing in the kitchen, Belle, the book's narrator, states "The shake-shake of maracas vibrates down to my toes" (Charles & Alcántara, 2021, n.p.). This engaging and enjoyable line is notable for its use of specific nouns: "maracas" and "toes" clearly convey key information to the reader. If author Tami Charles instead used vague, general nouns such as "musical instruments" and "body parts," we readers would not possess the same concrete understanding of the situation and the information being described. With the specific nouns, however, we can certainly understand the details of the scene.

As these examples from *Under the Mango Tree* and *Freedom Soup* illustrate, clear and specific nouns are important tools for effective writing. They establish concrete, easy-to-understand foundations for sentences and ensure that readers are able to understand the ideas in a piece of writing in the way that the author intended. Next, we'll take a look inside Kasey's classroom and see how she works with her students on the grammatical concept of nouns.

📷 Classroom Snapshot

Kasey's students were working on retelling fictional texts by identifying characters, setting, and events. She was teaching a whole-group lesson. She began the lesson by sharing the title of the read aloud, *Bear Says Thanks* (Wilson & Chapman, 2013). She explained to the students, "As you listen to the story, think about who the characters are, where the story takes place, and what happens in the story." Kasey read the book to the class and after reading the story, she said, "Now we are going to retell the story. As we retell the story, we are also going to learn about nouns. Nouns are words that refer to people, places, or things." Kasey then wrote each category of nouns on the board and began discussing examples of people, places, and things. She called on students who were eager to share their own examples for each category and Kasey added the examples to the lists.

Now that students had an idea of what nouns are, she asked them to think back to the story, *Bear Says Thanks*. She asked students, "What is the setting in the story?" Students raised their hands and Kasey called on a student who answered, "In the cave." Kasey replied, "Yes! The setting of the story is in the cave and the cave is a place." Kasey wrote "place" and under it, "cave." Next, Kasey asked, "Who are the characters in the story?" Students raised their hands excitedly to share and as they shared Kasey wrote the characters from the story in a new column on the board and then wrote "animals" at the top of the category and explained that sometimes the characters in a story are animals instead of people. She then asked students to recall events from the story. A student shared, "Hare brought muffins for Bear." Kasey wrote "muffins" in a new column. Another student shared, "Badger brought Bear some fish after he went fishing at the fishin' hole." Kasey added "fish" to the list in the new column and "fishin' hole" under "place." Students continued to share about other things that happened in the story, Kasey added "nuts," "pears," "food," "tree," and "quilt" to the list and wrote "things" at the top of the category. Kasey reviewed with the class each of the noun categories and the information they shared from the story. Kasey explained to the students, "Authors use nouns to help readers better understand what is happening in the story. These are nouns that the author used in the story we read. We are able to understand who and what Bear is thankful for."

After the lesson, students got out their writing journal. Kasey modeled writing the categories, people, places, things, and animals on the board for students to see. She explained, "Now that we have learned about what nouns are and looked at how authors use them in their writing, we are going to create lists of different nouns." She modeled drawing a teacher under "people" and wrote "t" for teacher and then asked students to draw and write nouns under each category. As students began working on their lists, Kasey walked around the room to assist students. Some students were only drawing pictures under each category. Other students were able to draw and write the beginning sound of the word or sound out the word phonetically. As students continued to work, Kasey asked some students to dictate their drawing and wrote the corresponding word under the pictures if they were not able to write yet or to clarify a picture. Students worked for about 15 to 20 minutes on their noun lists. Kasey signaled to students to stop writing and asked them to put their pencils and crayons down so they could share their writing. Kasey started with the first category and asked students to share some of their ideas. She continued through each category and called on students to share their ideas with the class. After students finished sharing, Kasey closed the lesson by saying, "Today we learned about what nouns are, how and why authors use them, and identified nouns through our retelling of *Bear Says Thanks*. As we continue to work on our reading and writing skills, see if you can identify nouns in the books you read or use nouns in your writing."

Recommendations for Teaching Students About Nouns

In this section, we describe a step-by-step instructional process that we recommend teachers use when teaching their early elementary students about the grammatical concept of nouns. This process is designed to help students understand what this concept is, why it is important, and how to apply it to their own writing. The steps of the instructional process are as follows:

1. Introduce important information about nouns to students.
2. Show students how published authors use nouns in their works.
3. Talk with students about the nouns those authors use and why they use them.
4. Support students as they create examples of nouns.
5. Ask students to reflect on why nouns are important.

By using this instructional process, you'll support students as they engage with the grammatical concept of nouns in increasingly reflective ways that help them understand how this concept is an important tool for effective writing. Now, let's take a look at each of these instructional steps in more detail.

Step One: Introduce Important Information About Nouns to Students

We recommend beginning this instructional process by introducing some key information about nouns to students. At this stage, it's important not to overwhelm students with a great deal of explanations and definitions, but instead to focus on some fundamental details that will represent a foundation for the rest of the work students do with this grammatical concept. Specifically, we suggest holding a mini-lesson with students in which you describe what nouns are and provide students with examples of common and proper nouns that represent different noun types (such as people, places, things, and ideas). Figures 1.1 and 1.2 provide useful information from which you can draw when explaining key noun information to your students: Figure 1.1 gives an overview of nouns and Figure 1.2 lists common nouns and corresponding proper nouns. As you discuss examples and explanations like these with your students, we encourage you to write key pieces of information on chart paper that you then hang up in your classroom for students to access later. This introductory mini-lesson is meant to introduce students to the topic and build a foundation on which they will draw throughout the instructional process and beyond. By posting key ideas around the class for future reference, you'll send a message to your students that they will continue to learn about this concept and are not expected to memorize information immediately. A clear mini-lesson on fundamental features of nouns and the display of corresponding resources will help position students to continue to think in increasingly thoughtful ways throughout this instructional process.

Step Two: Show Students How Published Authors Use Nouns in Their Works

After you've established foundational knowledge for students by introducing important information about nouns, we encourage you to provide your students with authentic examples of this grammatical concept by showing them how published authors use nouns in their works. To do so, we recommend conducting read alouds with students using books that are relevant and engaging to them and identifying key nouns used in those works. (While reading a book out loud, it's a great idea to also display it using a document camera so that students can see the nouns you're identifying.) For example, if you read to your students the following passage from the book *All Because You Matter* (Charles & Collier, 2020), you could highlight nouns such as "knapsack," "backs," and "ancestors": "Long before you took your place in this world, you were dreamed of, like a knapsack full of wishes, carried on the backs of your ancestors as they created empires, pyramids, legacies" (n.p.). This example—and others from similarly excellent and purposefully selected mentor texts—will provide your students with authentic examples of how authors use nouns in their works. By looking at published uses of nouns like the ones in this excerpt from *All Because You Matter*, students can see how this concept is used in real-world situations. In addition, looking at these examples of nouns will prepare students for the next step of the instructional process, in which they will think further about the importance of this concept to effective writing.

Step Three: Talk With Students About the Nouns Those Authors Use and Why They Use Them

Now that you've shown students authentic examples of nouns in engaging and accessible mentor texts, the next step is to talk with students about the nouns those authors used and why they used them. To do so, we recommend returning to each noun you highlighted in the previous section and discussing two key pieces of information about each one: 1) what makes it a noun and 2) the impact of that noun on the piece. For example, when talking with students about the noun "knapsack" in the phrase "like a knapsack full of wishes" in *All Because You Matter* (Charles & Collier, 2020, n.p.), we suggest first discussing why "knapsack" is a noun. When having this discussion, you might identify "knapsack" as an example of a noun and then ask students to help you identify the noun category—people, place, thing, or idea—in which it fits. The graphic organizer depicted in Figure 1.3 can guide you as you do this. As you talk with students about the nouns in a mentor text and the categories associated with them, you can complete the graphic organizer with them to provide a visual representation of this information. (A reproducible version of this graphic organizer is also available in Appendix B.)

Example of Noun in the Mentor Text	Category to Which the Noun Belongs (Person, Place, Thing, or Idea)

Figure 1.3 Noun Category Graphic Organizer

Once you and your students have identified nouns in a mentor text and the categories to which they belong, we suggest engaging students in a conversation about the impact of that noun on the piece of writing. For example, after discussing the fact that "knapsack" is a noun and that it is an example of a thing, you can ask your students "What is the use of a knapsack?" Students can then share their ideas on this question; as you listen to their responses, you can emphasize how a knapsack is used to carry things, which in this case holds the wishes that are so important to the sentence. After that, to extend the activity even further, you might even talk with students about the specificity of the noun "knapsack," pointing out that author Tami Charles's use of a specific noun helps the reader understand the information exactly as the author originally intended. By describing why a particular word or phrase is an example of a noun and the impact of that particular noun on the piece of writing, we can help our students develop their understanding of nouns and the purposeful ways authors use that concept.

Step Four: Support Students as They Create Examples of Nouns

At this stage in the instructional process, students can apply their noun-related ideas and understanding by working to create their own examples of this concept. To get students started on this step, you might recap what they've done up to that point in their work on the concept and then indicate what is to come next with a statement like this one: "We've been working really hard on nouns lately! We've talked about what nouns are, looked at published examples of them, and talked about why the author of the story we read used the nouns they did. Now, it's your turn to create your own nouns!" When students work to create their own examples, they can do so in a variety of ways associated with their individual literacy levels, such as creating a single noun, writing a sentence with at least one noun in it, dictating to the teacher a single noun or full sentence, or drawing a picture that includes a person, place, thing, or idea and verbally explaining what noun is present in that image. All of these forms of expression are methods that students can use to display their understanding of the grammatical tool of nouns. As students continue to develop as writers, they can move from one method of communication to another based on their comfort levels.

As students create their nouns, we encourage you to check in with them individually, holding one-on-one writing conferences in which you ask them to tell you about the noun they created. In these conferences, you might ask your students follow-up questions such as how they know the noun they're creating is in fact a noun, which of the noun categories it aligns with, and why they chose to create that particular noun. If students are struggling with creating a noun or have created something that is not a noun, you can refer them to the explanations and information you shared at the beginning of this instructional process and the published examples they examined. These explanations can support students who may benefit from additional guidance.

Step Five: Ask Students to Reflect on Why Nouns Are Important

After students have created examples of nouns in ways that align with their individual writing and literacy levels, we recommend concluding this instructional process by asking them to reflect on the importance of nouns to effective writing. To do this, you can ask your students questions such as "Why is it important that authors use nouns in their writing?" and "What would a piece of writing be like if an author didn't use any nouns?" If you feel students are also ready to think about the importance of specific and clear nouns to effective writing, you can also ask them to consider the significance of this topic with a question such as "How do specific and clear nouns make a piece of writing as strong as possible?" By asking students to reflect on the impact of nouns on effective writing, we can help them develop a lasting understanding of this concept. When we build students' awareness not only of what a concept is, but also why it is an important tool that authors purposefully and strategically apply to their works, we help them develop a metacognitive understanding of the impact of that concept that they can continue to apply to the writing they do in the future.

Final Thoughts on Nouns

In this section, we summarize major points from this chapter, including what nouns are, why they are important to effective writing, and instructional ideas for teaching early elementary school students about this concept:

- ◆ Nouns are words used to refer to people, places, things, or ideas.
- ◆ Nouns can be either common or proper: common nouns refer to general people, places, things or ideas, while proper nouns refer to specific examples.
- ◆ Nouns are essential tools for effective writing: authors use nouns in their works to convey to their readers the people, places, things, and ideas they are discussing.
- ◆ To maximize the effectiveness of noun use, authors often use the most clear and specific nouns they can.

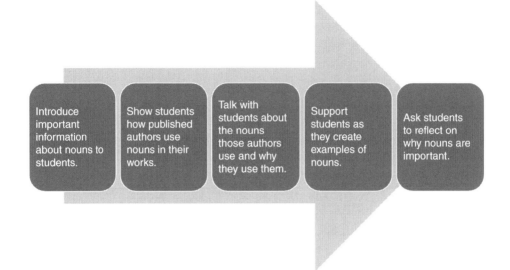

Figure 1.4 Noun Instructional Flowchart

◆ When teaching early elementary students about the concept of
nouns, we recommend following this instructional process:
- Introduce important information about nouns to students.
- Show students how published authors use nouns in their works.
- Talk with students about the nouns those authors use and why
they use them.
- Support students as they create examples of nouns.
- Ask students to reflect on why nouns are important.

Figure 1.4 depicts this process in an easy-to-follow flowchart.

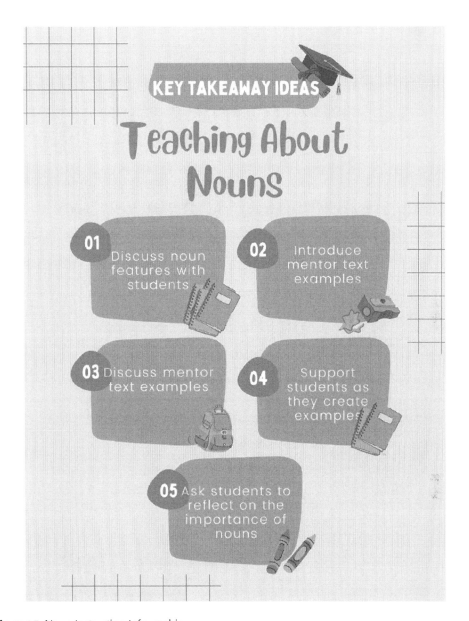

Figure 1.5 Noun Instruction Infographic

This infographic provides an accessible visual representation of a mentor-text-based instructional process to use when teaching students about nouns. It indicates that teachers should discuss noun features with their students, introduce mentor text examples of this concept, discuss those mentor text examples, support students as they create their own examples, and finally ask students to reflect on the importance of nouns. This image is also available on the book's website as down-loadable Support Material.

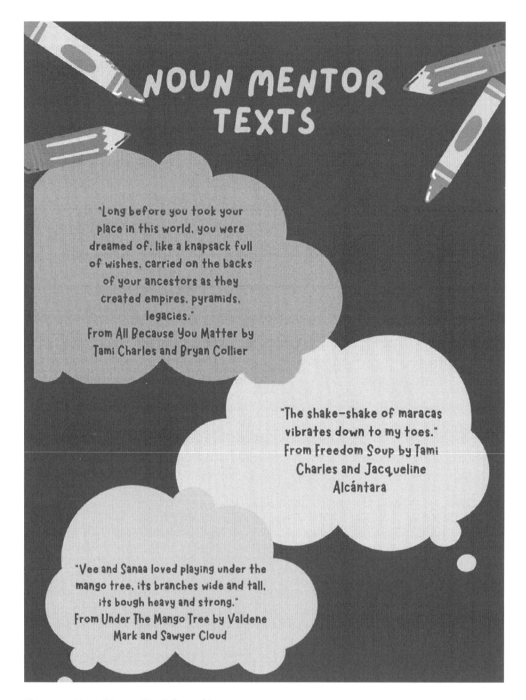

Figure 1.6 Noun Mentor Text Infographic

This infographic provides a visually appealing representation of key noun mentor texts discussed in this chapter. It contains examples of effectively used nouns from the published texts *All Because You Matter* by Tami Charles and Bryan Collier, *Freedom Soup* by Tami Charles and Jacqueline Alcántara, and *Under the Mango Tree* by Valdene Mark and Sawyer Cloud. This image is also available on the book's website as downloadable Support Material.

2 🔧

Getting Active

The Impact of Verbs

What Are Verbs?

In this chapter, we'll look closely at another grammatical element that is essential to effective writing: the concept of verbs. Verbs are typically used to show a physical action or a state of being. Let's take a look at each of these verb uses.

Verbs That Show Physical Action

Many verbs are used to express a physical action that someone or something performed, such as "celebrated," "ate," or "played." Some examples of sentences that contain these action verbs are "The winning team **celebrated** its victory," "The friends **ate** cake at the party," and "The children **played** basketball on the playground." Through action verbs, authors can communicate exactly what someone or something did. In the 2019 book *Fry Bread*, author Kevin Noble Maillard uses the action verb "mold" in the statement "Hands mold the dough" (Maillard & Martinez-Neal, 2019, n.p.). This verb shows the action that the hands described perform to create the bread discussed in the book.

Verbs That Show a State of Being

In addition to conveying a physical action, verbs can also be used to express a state of being, such as a personality trait, feeling, or other characteristic. Examples of these verbs are forms of the verb "be" (such as "am," "is," "are," "was," "were," "being," and "been") and verbs that relate to the senses (such "looks," "sounds," "smells," "tastes," and "feels"). Some ways these words

DOI: 10.4324/9781003302209-3

Verb Type	Description	Examples	How It Can Look in a Sentence
Verbs that show physical action	These verbs are used to express a physical action or an act that someone or something performed.	Celebrated Ate Played	The winning team **celebrated** its victory. The friends **ate** cake at the party. The children **played** basketball on the playground.
Verbs that show a state of being	These verbs are used to express a state of being, such as a personality trait, feeling, or other characteristic.	Forms of the verb "be" (such as "am," "is," "are," "was," "were," "being," and "been") Verbs that relate to the senses (such "looks," "sounds," "smells," "tastes," and "feels")	The students **are** intelligent. The pie **tastes** delicious.

Figure 2.1 Key Verb Information

can appear in sentences could be "The students **are** intelligent," "The teacher **is** in the classroom," "The pie **tastes** delicious," and "The music **sounds** great." In each of these instances, the verb doesn't represent a physical thing that someone does, but rather some type of attribute that relates to the noun being described. In the book *Not So Different*, author Cyana Riley (2020) writes "Everyone is different . . ." (n.p.). In this sentence, Riley uses the verb "is" to convey the attribute and state of being that she is discussing. Instead of depicting a physical action, this verb illustrates an important characteristic.

Figure 2.1 summarizes key information about verbs that show actions and those that show states of being.

Now that we've explored features and examples of verbs that show actions and those that convey a state of being, let's look in detail at why verbs are an essential tool for effective writing.

Why Verbs Are Important to Effective Writing

Verbs are essential tools for writers to understand and use in their works because of the ways they express an action or an important state of being. In Chapter 1, we discussed how nouns indicate the people, places, things, and ideas authors are discussing; verbs work in tandem with nouns by conveying to the reader what those nouns are doing or other significant information about them. Don and Jenny Killgallon (2010) describe the impact of verbs by calling them the "narrating tools" (p. 61) and explaining that authors use verbs in their works to narrate what is taking place in a piece of writing. For example, in the book *Jabari Jumps*, author and illustrator Gaia Cornwall (2020) uses the verbs "spread" and "bent" in a sentence describing children jumping off a diving board: "They spread their arms and bent their knees" (n.p). These verbs provide a clear narration and description of the actions discussed in the sentence. This same sense of narration also applies when authors use verbs that show a state of being. For instance, in the book *Children Make Terrible Pets*, author and illustrator Peter Brown (2010) uses the verb "were" to narrate important information in the sentence "Lucy and Squeaker were inseparable" (n.p.). In this excerpt, Brown shares a key attribute of these two individuals; the verb use in the text makes this possible.

The Impact of Strong Verbs

To maximize the effectiveness of their narration, authors often use verbs that clearly and effectively express what a noun is doing. This is especially true with verbs that convey action—for these verbs to illustrate to the reader exactly how an action is being performed, it's important for that verb to provide specific information about what was done. These verbs, called strong verbs because of the way they strengthen the reader's understanding of exactly how an action was performed (Robb, 2001), are key components of effective verb use. Because strong verbs allow readers to clearly imagine particular actions taking place, they ensure that readers are able to understand events exactly as authors intend them (Robb, 2001).

For example, instead of writing that a character "said" something, an author might use a stronger verb replacement such as "whispered," "shouted," or "cheered." These strong verbs clearly convey the way the action was performed, providing much more specificity than the weaker and vaguer version "said." While something can be "said" in a variety of ways, stronger versions of this verb provide much more clarity. Published authors use strong verbs to enhance the clarity and detail of their works. In the book *Milo Imagines the World* (de la Peña & Robinson, 2021), author Matt de la Peña uses a strong verb in the excerpt "Milo slips aboard" (n.p.). The verb "slips" is particularly strong and effective in this passage because it captures exactly how Milo boarded a subway train. If de la Peña had used a weaker verb here, such as "goes" or "moves," readers wouldn't know how he boarded the train. However, the strong verb "slips" illustrates exactly how he did it.

Weak Verbs	Strong Verb Replacements
Said	Whispered Shouted Cheered Grumbled
Went	Sprinted Charged Galloped Skipped
Looked	Stared Glanced Peered Gazed

Figure 2.2 Weak Verbs and Strong Verb Replacements

Figure 2.2 identifies some weak verbs and strong verbs that can be used to replace them.

Now, let's take a look inside Kasey's kindergarten classroom and see how she works with her students on the writing tool of verbs.

📷 Classroom Snapshot

Kasey had been working hard on incorporating intentional writing practice for her students throughout each day. Kasey's goal for her students was to sound out words phonetically to write sentences independently. Although students may recognize and identify all letters and letter sounds, it takes time for them to become confident enough to apply that knowledge into writing sentences. Once students were able to master this, Kasey worked on fine-tuning sentences, including spacing between words, capitalization, punctuation, and neat handwriting and correct letter formation. When students worked on writing, Kasey would frequently remind students to "add more" to their writing. Rather than, "I see a dog.", a student might add more by writing, "I see a black dog with spots." or "I see a black and white dog running down the street."

When Kasey taught the lesson about nouns previously, she tied the instruction into a reading skill that students were working on because students' writing wasn't as developed at that time. Since then, most students in her class had really progressed in their writing and were able to write two to three simple sentences independently. Kasey was confident it was the perfect opportunity to dig into grammar and further students' understanding of what makes good writing. Now the focus was using mentor texts solely to support students' understanding of grammar and writing.

Kasey began the lesson by reviewing what students had learned previously about nouns. She explained that not only do sentences contain a noun (person, place, or thing) but also a verb. Kasey used Figure 2.1 to explain what verbs are and examples of each. While Kasey explained the two types of verbs to students, verbs that show action and verbs that show a state of being, she decided to focus more on action verbs since students would be able to identify and apply these into their writing more easily. Kasey explained that the action verbs express the physical action that someone or something performed. She gave another example to students, "The dog ran down the street. What did the dog do?" the students replied, "ran." Kasey replied, "Very good! Who? . . . the dog, that is our noun and ran is our verb. Sentences contain a noun and a verb." She proceeded to give the students a few more examples, "The boy jumped in the pool. I rode my bike to the park." After she gave each example, she stopped and asked, "What did the boy do? What did I do?" Students identified the verbs in each sentence. Kasey then used Figure 2.2 to explain the difference between a weak verb and a strong verb. Kasey gave a few more examples to the students and explained that strong verbs give the reader a better understanding of how someone or something performed an action.

Now that students had an understanding of verbs, Kasey explained that students were going to listen to the story *Jabari Jumps* (Cornwall, 2020) and identify verbs that the author uses. Kasey stopped after the first few pages to highlight some of the verbs the author used to explain what Jabari saw at the pool: watched, climb, walked, stood, spread, bent, sprang, dove. Kasey said, "The author uses these verbs to paint a picture for us, the readers, of exactly what Jabari sees. These verbs help us understand each step of the process the kids at the pool took to dive off the diving board. Imagine if the author said, "The kids jumped off the diving board." This doesn't explain how the kids did it. By "adding more" with verbs, readers are able to better understand the story and what is happening." Students listened to the rest of the story. After reading the story, Kasey reviewed some of the verbs from the story. Then, she referred back to Figure 2.2 to remind students about weak verbs and strong verbs. "Let's think about the verbs from the story. The author used strong verbs to explain how the kids jumped off the diving board. Rather than the author saying, 'The kids went off of the diving board.', the author broke down the process using strong verbs to explain the process."

After the lesson, it was time to apply what students had learned. Kasey said, "Today we learned about what verbs are and why authors use them. We are going to work together to create examples of verbs. I want you to think of a strong verb and a sentence using that verb." Students began raising their hands and sharing their ideas. As students shared, Kasey wrote the verbs and sentences on the board. Emma raised her hand and shared, "Collected! I collected the chocolate before mom saw it." Kasey replied, "Oh, you are sneaky! Very good. Rather than say, 'I got the chocolate before mom saw it.' you used a strong verb, collected." Another student shared, "Run . . . I run to my friend's house." Kasey replied, "Nice job! Run is a weak verb. Can you think of a strong verb that really helps me understand how you run to your friend's house?" The student replied, "Sprint!" Kasey replied, "Way to go, yes! I sprinted to my friend's house. That tells me that you ran fast to your friend's house because you were excited to see them!" Kasey encouraged students to continue to work on identifying verbs in read alouds and challenged them to use strong verbs in their writing.

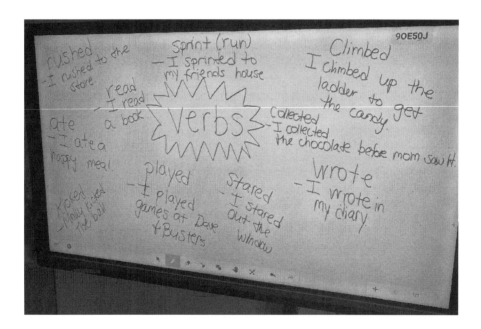

Recommendations for Teaching Students About Verbs

Here, we share a five-step instructional process for teachers to use when helping their early elementary students understand the concept of verbs, why using them is important to effective writing, and how to implement them in their own works. This process, which is designed to gradually release responsibility to students in purposeful and intentional ways, consists of the following steps:

1. Talk with students about the fundamental features of verbs.
2. Share with students published examples of effective verb use.
3. Discuss with students the verbs the authors use and the reasons they use them.
4. Help students as they create verbs in their own works.
5. Create opportunities for students to reflect on the importance of verbs.

Throughout this process, students will engage with the verbs in ways that establish their understanding of this writing tool and help them consider the importance of verbs to effective writing. Let's take a look at the specifics of these instructional steps.

Step One: Talk With Students About the Fundamental Features of Verbs

We encourage you to begin this instructional process by introducing students to key information about verbs, conducting an introductory mini-lesson in which you talk with them about the fundamental features and attributes of this concept. To do so, we recommend first connecting to the information about nouns discussed in the previous chapter to contextualize verbs and show how they align with material students have already learned. For example, you might provide students with an explanation such as "When we talked about nouns, we talked about how they are used to name things. A lot of times, we use verbs along with nouns. We can use verbs to show what those nouns do. Verbs can show what something or someone does, like 'sprint' or 'jump.' They can also show something about a noun, like if we said 'My teacher is in the classroom' or 'My teacher seems nice.' Those are all types of verbs."

As you share key information about verbs during this mini-lesson, we encourage you to record essential points about this concept on chart paper and post those resources around the classroom for future reference. On this chart paper, you can write a brief explanation of what verbs are, describe the types of information they provide, and list some examples of verbs that express physical actions and those that show states of being. Depending on your students' familiarity and comfort with verbs, you might also introduce the concept of strong verbs to students by distinguishing between weak and strong verbs and providing them with examples of strong verbs that can replace commonly used weak verbs. In this opening mini-lesson, it's important not to overwhelm students with a great deal of information about verbs—their awareness of and familiarity with the concept will increase throughout the process. Instead, the most important feature of this introductory session is to orient students to this writing tool by establishing the foundational knowledge that you'll build on throughout this instructional process.

Step Two: Share With Students Published Examples of Effective Verb Use

Once you've introduced students to key features of verbs, we recommend making connections to the authentic use of this concept by showing them how published authors use verbs in their works. This instructional step builds off the previous one: it provides a real-world application of the information, explanations, and examples shared in the opening part of the process. To convey to students how published authors utilize verbs in their works, we recommend reading a book to students and working with them to identify the verbs used in the text. We encourage you to use picture books that your students will find accessible and engaging for this activity to make the concept accessible and interesting for your early elementary grade students. As you read the book, you can first identify examples of verbs for students; after students have seen you do this, we recommend then further encouraging their involvement by asking them for examples of verbs they see in the texts. This process can gradually give students additional ownership of their learning.

For example, in the book *I Dream of Popo* (Blackburne & Kuo, 2021), author Livia Blackburne effectively uses verbs to express important actions and narrate the story's events. If you read this text to your students, you can call attention to the sentence "I walk with Popo in the park, squeezing her finger in my chubby palm" (n.p.) and identify the verbs "walk" and "squeezing." As you continue to read the book aloud to your students, we suggest pausing as you read and asking students to share examples of verbs they've noticed. This instructional activity will provide students with knowledge of ways that authors authentically use verbs in their writing. In addition, it will prepare them to think further about why the author chose to use those verbs—the next step in this instructional process.

Step Three: Discuss With Students the Verbs the Authors Use and the Reasons They Use Them

This step further develops students' understanding of the grammatical concept of verbs by engaging them in discussions of their features and impacts. To engage students in this activity, we recommend returning to each verb identified during the previous read aloud activity and discussing the following information about each one: 1) what makes it a verb and 2) why the author may have chosen to use that verb. For instance, when discussing the verbs "walk" and "squeezing" in the sentence "I walk with Popo in the park, squeezing her finger in my chubby palm" (Blackburne & Kuo, 2021, n.p.) from *I Dream of Popo*, we recommend first talking with students about why each one is a verb. To do so, we suggest returning to the information discussed in the initial mini-lesson about the features of verbs and talking with students about the type of verb each one is, pointing out that both of these verbs show actions that the narrator performed in the story.

Next, we recommend building on students' understanding by helping them think about why the author may have chosen to use each verb. For example, when discussing the verb "squeezing" with students, you might ask them questions such as "Why do you think the author wrote 'squeezing' in this sentence?" and "How does this verb help the author tell the story?" As students respond, you can help them think about ways that the verb "squeezing" shows readers what the narrator was doing when taking a walk with Popo. In addition, you might encourage students to think about how this verb shows readers exactly how the action was performed. By using the word "squeezing" instead of a more general or vague description, the author uses a strong verb that helps them tell the story in a clear and specific way. These questions and their corresponding discussion can activate students' higher-order thinking skills by helping them understand the features of verbs and the reasons why authors might use certain verbs in their works.

Figure 2.3 is a resource that can facilitate your discussions with students about the verbs authors use and the reasons they use them. It provides spaces for you to identify verbs in a text, what makes it a verb, and why the author may have chosen to use that verb. We recommend completing this chart with students as you discuss these ideas; by filling out the chart with them, you'll involve them in the analysis and provide a visual representation of these ideas. (A reproducible version of this graphic organizer is also available in Appendix B.)

Verb	What Makes It a Verb?	Why Might the Author Have Chosen to Use That Verb?

Figure 2.3 Verb Analysis Chart

Step Four: Help Students as They Create Verbs in Their Own Works

Now that students have looked at key verb features, noticed their usage in published writing, and thought about why the author used those verbs, the students can take on increased responsibility in this instructional process by creating verbs in their own works. To prepare students to do this, we recommend giving students a combination review discussion and pep talk that recaps the key features of verbs and excites students to use this concept in their works. For example, after reminding students of the verb explanations and examples they've discussed, you might tell them "Now it's time to try this out on your own. You're going to create your own description that uses a verb. You'll be using a verb to show important information about what someone does or something about them just like the authors we studied did in their descriptions!" We encourage you to offer your students a wide range of options to utilize verbs in their works: for instance, they can create written narrations, draw a picture (with or without accompanying text), or dictate a description of an action to the teacher. These opportunities all provide students with ways to practice verbs and become increasingly familiar with this concept and how it is used to create strong narration.

As students work on creating their descriptions, we encourage you to check in with them to monitor their understanding and provide them with any support they need. For example, when conferring with students on their progress, we suggest asking them to show you the verb they used in their work and to talk with you about the information that verb provides. As students share this information, you can help them clarify any confusion they have about their verb use. In addition, you can use this conversation to encourage students to think even further about the features of verbs: you might ask them whether the verb they used describes an action or a state of being and why they chose to use the verb they did. These conferences can also be good opportunities to remind students about strong verbs and the reasons writers use them. If a student uses a weaker or vaguer verb like "said" or "went," you can use this meeting to help them think about stronger verbs that can provide readers with more specific detail and information. By holding these individualized conferences, you'll be able to provide students with personalized feedback as they utilize verbs in the descriptions they create.

Step Five: Create Opportunities for Students to Reflect on the Importance of Verbs

This concluding instructional step encourages students to think metacognitively about the impact of verbs on effective writing. Reflecting on the importance of this writing tool can further develop students' understanding of what verbs are, why writers use them, and how they can impact the students' own works. To facilitate this reflection, we recommend asking students to consider reflection questions such as "Why are verbs important tools for effective writing?" and "What would a piece of writing that didn't use any verbs be like?" If you feel students are ready to reflect on the concept of strong verbs, you can also engage them in a reflection question on this topic such as "How do strong verbs make a piece of writing as good as it can possibly be?" Through reflection questions such as these, we can deepen students' awareness of the concept of strong verbs. The in-depth analysis and understanding that these reflective opportunities provide help students think carefully about the importance of verbs. Equipped with this knowledge, students can then feel increasingly comfortable using this concept in their works.

Final Thoughts on Verbs

In this section, we recap key insights from this chapter, such as important features of verbs, why they are important to effective writing, and instructional suggestions for teaching early elementary school students about them:

◆ Verbs are typically used to show a physical action or a state of being.
  – Verbs that express a physical action show what someone or something did, such as "celebrated," "ate," or "played."
  – Verbs that express a state of being show a personality trait, feeling, or other characteristic. Examples of these verbs are forms of the verb "be" (such as "am," "is," "are," "was," "were," "being," and "been") and verbs that relate to the senses (such "looks," "sounds," "smells," "tastes," and "feels").

◆ Verbs are essential tools for writers to understand and use in their works because of the ways they narrate (Killgallon & Killgallon, 2010) what is taking place in a piece of writing.

◆ To maximize the effectiveness of their narration, authors often use strong verbs: verbs that clearly and effectively express what a noun is doing.

◆ When teaching early elementary students about the concept of verbs, we recommend following this instructional process:

– Talk with students about the fundamental features of verbs.
– Share with students published examples of effective verb use.
– Discuss with students the verbs the authors use and the reasons they use them.
– Help students as they create verbs in their own works.
– Create opportunities for students to reflect on the importance of verbs.

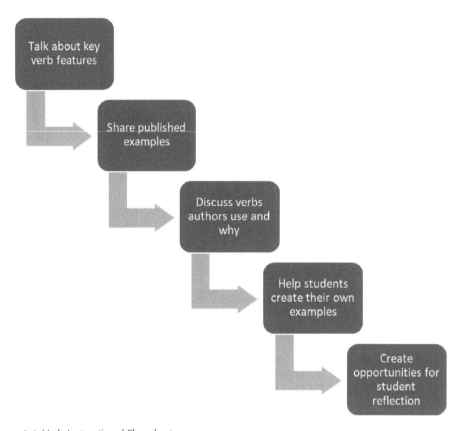

Figure 2.4 Verb Instructional Flowchart

Figure 2.4 depicts this process in any easy-to-follow flowchart.

This infographic provides an accessible visual representation of a mentor-text-based instructional process to use when teaching students about verbs.

This infographic provides a visually appealing representation of key verb mentor texts discussed in this chapter.

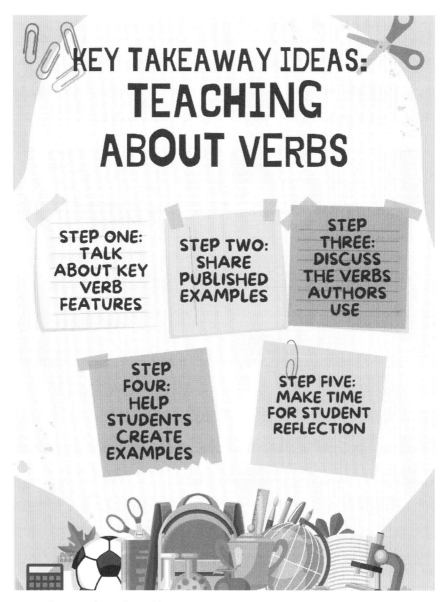

Figure 2.5 Verb Instruction Infographic

Figure 2.6 Verb Mentor Text Infographic

3 ⚙

Completing the Journey

Understanding and Constructing Complete Sentences

What Are Complete Sentences?

In Chapters 1 and 2, we looked at the key grammatical concepts of nouns and verbs, respectively. Now, we'll examine how these two tools work together to create an important component of effective writing: complete sentences. While a complete sentence can take a variety of forms, the essential features of one is that it contains a subject and a verb, expresses a complete thought, and concludes with end punctuation. (We'll look in detail at end punctuation in Chapter 4.) Complete sentences can be very short and contain a subject, verb, and nothing or little else (such as "Julie ran.") or they can have a number of additional features that add more detail (such as "Yesterday morning, Julie ran through the field.") The amount of detail and information in a sentence depends on how much context the author wants to convey to readers. For instance, the two previous sentences about Julie running both contain the same subject and verb, but have different levels of detail and context. In some situations, authors might provide a lot of description information; in others, they might limit this information. Either way, as long as the sentence contains a subject and verb, expresses a complete thought, and concludes with end punctuation, it represents a complete sentence.

Figure 3.1 depicts some key information about complete sentences.

DOI: 10.4324/9781003302209-4

Grammatical Concept	Key Features of This Grammatical Concept	Examples of This Grammatical Concept	Explanation of Examples
Complete sentences	Contains a subject and a verb Expresses a complete thought Concludes with end punctuation	Julie ran. Yesterday morning, Julie ran through the field.	Although these sentences have differing levels of detail, they both possess the characteristics of complete sentences: each one contains a subject and verb, expresses a complete thought, and concludes with end punctuation.

Figure 3.1 Key Information About Complete Sentences

Let's now think further about complete sentences by examining why they are important tools for effective writing.

Why Complete Sentences Are Important to Effective Writing

Complete sentences are essential tools to effective communication because they convey ideas in clearly structured and easy-to-understand ways. Since each complete sentence contains a subject and verb, expresses a complete thought, and concludes with end punctuation, readers can identify these sentences when they read and determine when a writer has shared a complete idea for them to understand. If complete sentences didn't have these features, it would be much harder for readers to determine when writers had shared a fully formed idea. For example, in the book *We Are Water Protectors* (Lindstrom & Goade, 2020), the complete sentence "We come from water." (n.p.) expresses a fully formed idea about the character's belief about the importance of water. Although this sentence isn't long, it clearly shares the information that the author wants us readers to know and includes the characteristics of complete sentences.

An example of a longer complete sentence from a published text is the line "I have eyes that kiss in the corners and glow like warm tea." (n.p.) from the book *Eyes That Kiss in the Corners* (Ho & Ho, 2021). This sentence, like other complete sentences, contains a subject ("I") and a main verb ("have"), expresses a complete thought, and concludes with end punctuation. By looking at it, we can see an example of a way that complete sentences can be structured and the amount of detail they can have. In the passage, author Joanna Ho uses the descriptive phrases "that kiss in the corners" and "glow like warm tea" to describe the character's eyes and elaborate on the fundamental information in the sentence. The combination of these details and the sentence's essential elements clearly conveys to readers the information that the book's narrator shares about her eyes. If this passage contained its descriptive information but lacked its subject and verb, it would not be a complete sentence and would not clearly communicate its key message to the reader.

These examples from *We Are Water Protectors* and *Eyes That Kiss in the Corners* demonstrate the impact of complete sentences on effective writing while also showing differing levels of detail and information that they can contain. Each sentence clearly conveys important information to the reader that helps them understand the story. If these excerpts were not complete sentences, it would be much harder for readers to comprehend the events and information that are relevant to the texts. However, by sharing this information through complete sentences, the authors create texts that are easy to understand. The variation in the length and the amount of detail in these complete sentence examples is important because it shows that complete sentences don't need to look one specific way. As long as they contain the essential attributes of a complete sentence, these sentences can have varying amounts of detail and information. Authors can choose how much additional information they would like to provide as they use complete sentences to share important ideas in their writing.

Now, we'll take a look inside Kasey's classroom and see how she helps her students understand the concept of complete sentences.

🖥 Classroom Snapshot

Kasey's students waited eagerly in anticipation of the lesson. One student asked, "Ms. Haddock, what are we going to learn today!?" Kasey began the lesson and explained, "We already learned about nouns and verbs. Today, we are going to talk about complete sentences. Complete sentences include a subject, a noun—person, place, or thing—and a verb. Complete sentences express a thought or idea and include ending punctuation. Kasey used Figure 3.1 to further explain the concept. She focused on the varying lengths of sentences and explained that even though one sentence is shorter than the other, they are still complete sentences. She referred to when she encourages students to "add more" to their sentences. "Rather than saying 'I like ice cream.' I can add more by saying 'I like chocolate ice cream with rainbow sprinkles.' Both of these have a subject and a verb and are complete sentences, but I added more details to my sentence in order for the reader to better understand what kind of ice cream I like. Longer sentences tend to have more details."

Kasey introduced the book *Bilal Cooks Daal* (Saeed & Syed, 2019) and explained, "This book is about a boy who cooks one of his favorite foods for his friends. As you listen to the story, look and listen for how the author uses complete sentences and sentences of varying lengths to share this story with us." Kasey began reading the book and stopped after the first few pages to highlight some of the sentences. "Notice, some sentences are longer than others but they all have a subject, who/what, and a verb, take off, wash, study." After reading about the spices, Kasey stopped again and highlighted the different parts of each sentence. Emma raised her hand and asked, "What is that thing that looks like a 9?" She pointed to the board and noticed the commas in the sentence, "Bilal breathes in the scent of turmeric, chili, cumin" (Saeed & Syed, 2019, n.p.). Kasey replied, "I am so glad that you noticed that, you are very observant! That is called a comma. Writers use a comma to separate a list of more than two things. Rather than using 'and' in between each word and sounding repetitive, you can use commas. Commas are a type of punctuation and we will talk about them later." Kasey went on to finish reading the rest of the story. After finishing the story, Kasey used Figure 3.2 to guide students through reflecting on the use of complete sentences in the story.

Now that students had a better understanding of what makes complete sentences and how writers use complete sentences to express their thoughts and ideas, it was time for students to apply their knowledge to their writing. The day before, students began brainstorming ideas for a writing assignment to send to their first-grade teacher. Students were focusing on writing "All About Me" for their teacher to get to know a little more about them. Students used a web with their name in the middle bubble and four bubbles branched off. In each bubble was a sentence starter: I can . . . I like . . . I am . . . I have. Students had already drawn a picture of something about them in each box. Kasey explained to students, "Yesterday, you drew a picture in each box to represent different things about yourself. Today, you are going to write a sentence about each one of those ideas. You are going to focus on writing complete sentences. I also want you to focus on 'adding more.'" Kasey pointed to an example of one of the bubbles that had a picture of a bike and said, "Would I write 'Ride my bike.' as a sentence?" Students quickly replied, "No!" Kasey responded, "Why not?" Terri raised her hand and said, "Because that is not a complete sentence." Kasey said, "Very good, 'Ride my bike.' is not a complete sentence. Remember, sentences need a subject (noun) and a verb. Who rides the bike? I can ride my bike." Students were given lined paper and used their brainstorming map to begin their writing. Since this was a graded assignment that was going to be used as a writing sample for first grade, it was completed independently without any teacher support. However, as students were working on their writing, Kasey walked around the room to observe student progress. Despite varying levels of development among the students, all students were able to write complete sentences on the topic. When students were finished, they brought their papers to Kasey and took turns reading aloud their writing to share with the class. When students were finished, Kasey revisited the goal of the lesson. "Today, we focused on writing complete sentences. You learned about what makes a complete sentence, we listened to a book to see how an author uses complete sentences to tell us a story, and you applied what you learned in your own writing to create sentences. As we continue to work on developing our writing, I encourage you to write complete sentences to clearly express your thoughts and ideas."

Recommendations for Teaching Students About Complete Sentences

Here, we present and discuss an instructional process designed for teachers to implement as they work with their students on the grammatical concept of complete sentences. The steps of this process are organized to help students understand what complete sentences are, why they are important tools for effective writing, and how to apply this concept to their own works. This process consists of the following five steps:

1. Introduce students to the key features of complete sentences.
2. Share published examples of complete sentences with students.
3. Discuss the published complete sentences with students.
4. Confer with students as they construct complete sentences.
5. Help students reflect on why complete sentences are important to effective writing.

Through the use of these instructional steps, you'll develop students' understanding of the grammatical concept of complete sentences and help them think analytically about the impact of these tools on strong and effective writing. Let's now check out each aspect of this process in more detail.

Step One: Introduce Students to the Key Features of Complete Sentences

This introductory step to the instructional process provides students with an overview of the fundamental features of complete sentences. When sharing this information with students, we encourage you to focus on introducing students to the concept of complete sentences and sharing with them key aspects of these sentences. One way to do this is to begin with an introductory statement that communicates to students what they'll be studying and why. For instance, you might say "Today we're going to begin thinking about an important part of effective writing: complete sentences. We're going to start by talking about what makes up a complete sentence. After that, in future days, we'll think about why writers use them and how we can use them on our own. First, let's get into the things that make a complete sentence complete." This introductory statement can give students an accessible point of entry into this concept; it communicates what they'll be thinking about that day and in future classes, as well as why they'll be exploring this topic.

Once you've explained to students that they'll be studying complete sentences, we recommend sharing key features of this concept. While doing so, we suggest referring to the concepts discussed in the book's first two chapters—nouns and verbs—and explaining how they play important roles in complete sentences. For example, you might say "We've already talked about nouns, which name things, and verbs, which can show what those nouns do. Complete sentences put this information together to share a complete thought. A complete sentence will have a subject, which is the main noun in the sentence, and a verb, which tells what that subject does. The subject, verb, and whatever other information the author wants to add, like some descriptive detail, will create a complete thought and finish with punctuation at the end. These things together make a complete sentence." As you share this explanation, we encourage you to record on a piece of chart paper the key features of complete sentences and corresponding examples listed in Figure 3.1. When you share the examples, we recommend emphasizing that complete sentences can be of different lengths as long as they contain the key features they need to have to be complete sentences. Once you've recorded this information on chart paper, we suggest posting it on the wall as you've done with the other grammatical concepts—this will provide students with a number of visual references to which they can return as they continue to apply the grammatical concepts you've taught them to their writing.

Step Two: Share Published Examples of Complete Sentences With Students

We recommend following up on the discussion of the features of complete sentences by sharing with students published examples of this grammatical concept. This activity is designed to highlight the authentic uses of complete sentences in published books—especially those books with which students are familiar. To do so, we suggest reading aloud to students from a book that they find engaging and is on their general reading level. While reading, we encourage you to display the text on a document camera if possible and point out examples of complete sentences in the book. Since a book will likely contain many complete sentences, you don't need to identify every single one. Instead, you might start the book by identifying the first few complete sentences and then identify examples that vary in their level of detail and information. By doing this, you can help students understand how much published authors utilize complete sentences in their works and the many forms these sentences take.

Before beginning this activity, you might remind students of the features of complete sentences and then explain that you'll be identifying some examples of this concept in the book you'll read. When informing students that you'll be calling their attention to these examples, you might say "As I read this book, I'll point out some complete sentences. I'll first point out some of the complete sentences at the beginning of the story. After that, I'll point out some complete sentences of different lengths to show you the different ways complete sentences can look." For instance, if you're reading to your students from the book *Bilal Cooks Daal* (Saeed & Syed, 2019), you might identify the shorter complete sentence "They take off their shoes." (n.p.) as well as the longer complete sentence "When Abu scoops out a cup of the bright yellow daal, it clatters in the bowl." (n.p.). As you note these sentences, it's a great idea to record them on a piece of chart paper in the classroom so that students have a variety of posted examples they can easily reference. By identifying these published sentences for students, you'll provide them with accessible and engaging examples of this important writing tool.

Step Three: Discuss the Published Complete Sentences With Students

Once students have seen published examples of complete sentences, the next step is to build on those identifications by discussing these sentences with them. To do so, we suggest talking about each sentence by focusing on two attributes: 1) what makes it a complete sentence and 2) why the complete sentence is important to the story. We recommend using the graphic organizer

Published Sentence	What Makes It a Complete Sentence	Why the Complete Sentence Is Important to the Story

Figure 3.2 Complete Sentence Discussion Graphic Organizer

in Figure 3.2 to facilitate these conversations: it contains space for the sentence, an explanation of why it is a complete sentence, and a discussion of the importance of that complete sentence to the story. (A reproducible version of this graphic organizer is also available in Appendix B.)

For example, when discussing the sentence "They take off their shoes." (n.p.) from *Bilal Cooks Daal* (Saeed & Syed, 2019) described in the previous recommendation, you can first lead students in a conversation about how it possesses the features of a complete sentence. In this discussion, we suggest working with students to identify the components of a complete sentence present in this excerpt: the subject and verb, the presence of end punctuation, and the fact that the sentence expresses a complete thought. A good way to begin this conversation is to remind the students of these features and then work with them to find these components. Depending on your students' level of comfort with the topic, you might model one of these identifications and then ask for student volunteers to find the other features. After you and your students have worked together to find these aspects, we recommend talking with them about the importance of this complete sentence to the story, highlighting what information the sentence provides, why that information is significant to the text, and how our understanding of what's taking place in the story might be different if we didn't know everything the sentence expresses. These discussions don't need to be particularly long or in depth: the objective is to help students think about the information in the sentence and to understand the importance of using complete sentences in effective writing.

Step Four: Confer With Students as They Construct Complete Sentences

At this stage in the instructional process, students can put the ideas they've learned about complete sentences into action by constructing their own examples. Before students do this, we recommend reviewing with students the features of complete sentences and the examples you've shared with them throughout this instructional process. As you remind students of the example sentences they've examined, it's a good idea to review the fact that complete sentences can take a variety of forms and have a range of levels of detail. You can encourage students to create sentences with the level of detail that aligns with that they'd like to express. Based on the individual attributes of your students and their specific comfort levels with this concept, we encourage you to provide a range of ways for your students to create these sentences, such as dictating a sentence that you write down, drawing an image and writing as much as a corresponding sentence as they're able, or writing a stand-alone sentence.

While students work on these sentences, we suggest holding individual conferences with them in which you check on their progress and provide them with individualized support. When you sit down with a student to confer with them, a good first step is to ask them to talk to you about the sentence they're creating and how they're constructing it: this will give you fundamental information about what the student wants to express and the modality they're using to express it. After that, we suggest following up by asking students to identify the key components of the sentence that make it a complete sentence and what complete thought it expresses. This will help students look for the essential attributes of complete sentences in their own work and create a natural instructional opportunity to address any information that might be missing. If there is anything that the student has said they want to express in the sentence that you don't feel is present, you can use this opportunity to suggest how they might include that information. Finally, we recommend asking the student what additional information they incorporated in the sentence that expands on the piece's fundamental components: this can help emphasize to students that authors can construct sentences in a range of ways that can include a variety of levels of detail.

Step Five: Help Students Reflect on Why Complete Sentences Are Important to Effective Writing

Once students have created their own examples of complete sentences, we encourage you to conclude the instructional process by helping them reflect on the importance of this concept to effective writing. To facilitate this reflection, we suggest first asking students "What is something that has stood out to you about complete sentences?" By responding to this question, students can take some time to consider what they've noticed and learned about during this instructional process. Asking this question also provides an opportunity to remind students of key concepts you've discussed with them about complete sentences. These reminders can maximize students' abilities to think carefully about the next question that we recommend asking: "Why are complete sentences important to effective writing?" When students reflect on this question, they will consider ideas such as how complete sentences help readers understand a piece of writing and the complete thoughts they express. Finally, as a follow-up question, we encourage you to ask students "How would writing be different if authors didn't use complete sentences?" This question encourages students to think even more deeply about the impact of this concept. Students might call attention to how writing might be hard to understand if writers used incomplete sentences instead of complete ones. As you ask students these questions, we recommend asking for their responses verbally and writing their responses on a projected screen or a piece of chart paper as they share. This can provide a visual record of their insights and can help them learn from each other's perspectives. As students share, we encourage you to comment on their insights and elaborate on key ideas so that they learn from each other about the impact of this concept.

Final Thoughts on Complete Sentences

In this final section, we summarize key ideas from this chapter, such as what complete sentences are, why they are important to effective writing, and recommended instructional practices for teaching early elementary students about this important writing tool:

- ◆ The key features of complete sentences are as follows:
  - – They contain a subject and verb.
  - – They express a complete thought.
  - – They conclude with end punctuation.
- ◆ As long as complete sentences include these features, they can contain a great deal of detail or very little detail.
- ◆ Complete sentences are essential tools to effective communication because they convey ideas in clearly structured and easy-to-understand ways.
- ◆ When teaching early elementary students about complete sentences, we recommend using this instructional process:
  - – Introduce students to the key features of complete sentences.
  - – Share published examples of complete sentences with students.
  - – Discuss the published complete sentences with students.
  - – Confer with students as they construct complete sentences.
  - – Help students reflect on why complete sentences are important to effective writing.

Figure 3.3 depicts this process in any easy-to-follow flowchart.

Figure 3.3 Complete Sentence Instructional Flowchart

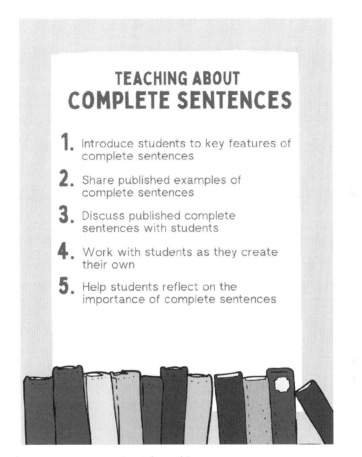

Figure 3.4 Complete Sentence Instruction Infographic

This infographic provides an accessible visual representation of a mentor-text-based instructional process to use when teaching students about complete sentences.

This infographic provides a visually appealing representation of key complete sentence mentor texts discussed in this chapter.

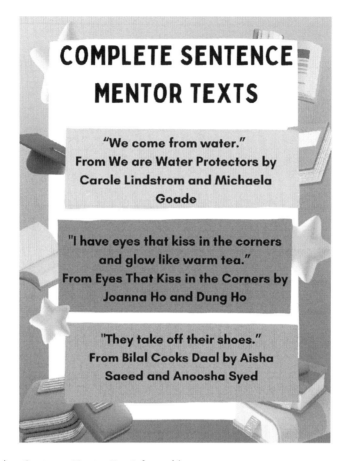

Figure 3.5 Complete Sentence Mentor Text Infographic

4

Finish Lines

How Writers Use End Punctuation

What Is End Punctuation?

In Chapter 3, we identified the essential attributes of complete sentences, explaining that a complete sentence contains a subject and a verb, expresses a complete thought, and concludes with end punctuation. In this chapter, we'll look closely at one of these components: end punctuation, which is punctuation that is used to indicate the completion of a sentence. There are three types of end punctuation: periods, question marks, and exclamation points. Let's take a look at each of these punctuation types individually.

Periods
Periods, which look like this (.) are punctuation marks used at the end of sentences that make straightforward statements. While there are a variety of statements that one might make in a sentence that ends in a period, these sentences are characterized by how they express an idea in a direct way without a great deal of emotion. For example, let's take the sentence "The game is today." This sentence expresses the statement in a clear and direct way and does not convey a lot of emotion about the situation.

Question Marks
Question marks look like this (?) and are used at the end of sentences that ask direct questions. The sentence "When is the game?" asks a direct question and uses a question mark at its conclusion. Sometimes the question aspect of

DOI: 10.4324/9781003302209-5

Punctuation Form	Explanation	Examples
Period (.)	Punctuation mark used at the end of sentences that make straightforward statements.	The game is today.
Question mark (?)	Punctuation mark used at the end of sentences that ask direct questions.	When is the game? The game is today, correct?
Exclamation point (!)	Punctuation mark used to express a great deal of emotion in a sentence.	The game is today!

Figure 4.1 End Punctuation Information

a sentence is separated from the rest of it, such as in the sentence "The game is today, correct?" While the specific structure of that sentence is somewhat different from the previous example "When is the game?," both sentences end with question marks because, in each case, the speaker or author is asking a question.

Exclamation Points

Exclamation points, which look like this (!) are used to express a great deal of emotion in a sentence. For example, we can take the sentence "The game is today." from the earlier section on periods and add emotion to it with an exclamation point. This sentence would read "The game is today!" and would express a much different attitude than the version that ends with a period. This form of end punctuation shows that a speaker or author wants to express a statement in a way that clearly conveys strong emotions.

Figure 4.1 identifies key information about these three end punctuation forms.

Why End Punctuation Is Important to Effective Writing

The forms of end punctuation are important to effective writing because they guide readers' understanding of the information in a sentence. When writers decide whether to conclude a sentence with a period, a question mark, or an exclamation point, they are communicating to readers how to make sense of that sentence. For example, when an author ends a sentence with a question mark, they are letting readers know that a question is being asked in that sentence. If they didn't conclude the sentence with a question mark, readers would likely be confused as they try to understand it. For instance, if the previously used sentence "When is the game?" ended with a period instead of a question mark (and read "When is the game."), it would be difficult to understand. While the language in the sentence would suggest that the writer or speaker is asking a question, the punctuation would not indicate this. By using a question mark, an author would clearly communicate to readers that the sentence expresses a question. One example of an effective and purposefully used question mark in a published text is found in the following sentence from *More than a Princess* (Coleman et al., 2020): "What else would you like to explore, little one?" (n.p.). The question mark at the conclusion of this sentence lets readers know that there is a question being asked here. Without this specific end punctuation, it would be difficult to understand the message of the sentence.

Similarly, the end punctuation marks of periods and exclamation points play important roles in helping readers understand what is being expressed in a sentence. While an exclamation point conveys excitement or emotion in a sentence, a period shows that the information is meant to be expressed in a more straightforward way. For instance, in the book *How to Wear a Sari* (Khiani & Lew-Vriethoff, 2021), author Darshana Khiani purposefully uses both of these forms of end punctuation to convey the messages and tones of particular sentences. Khiani uses a period at the conclusion of the sentence "First, you need to find the perfect Sari." (n.p.) to communicate a straightforward tone. If this sentence ended with an exclamation point, it would express a different feeling to readers than it currently does. At another point in the book, Khiani strategically utilizes an exclamation point to help readers understand the information in the way it was intended. In the sentence "Gorgeous choice!" (n.p.), the concluding exclamation point shows the emotion that corresponds with the statement. Without this important end punctuation, readers would not know to read the text with the level of emotion that the author intended.

As these examples illustrate, the end punctuation marks of periods, question marks, and exclamation points are important writing tools. By using them, writers provide their readers with signals that express how to read and make sense of the information in a text. These signals ensure that readers understand the sentences in the ways the writers intended them and that they are able to accurately interpret their information. Now that we've explored the importance of these end punctuation forms to effective writing, let's take a look at how Kasey teaches her students about these concepts.

📷 Classroom Snapshot

Kasey began the lesson by saying, "Yesterday, we learned about complete sentences. Complete sentences contain ending punctuation. When you write sentences, what do you put at the end of your sentence?" Students answered, "A period!" Kasey replied, "That's right! Today, we are going to learn about ending punctuation. That is a big word, can you say 'Punctuation?'" Students said the word aloud and Kasey replied, "Very good! Ending punctuation is what we put at the end of a sentence. There are three different types of ending punctuation and each one has a different purpose." Kasey directed students to look at the board, where she used Figure 4.1 to explain the different types of ending punctuation. When Kasey read the examples of each type of punctuation, she made sure to emphasize her expression appropriately and explained that the ending punctuation indicates to the reader how the message is conveyed. We adjust our voice and expression when we read different types of ending punctuation.

Kasey showed the students the cover of the book *Parts* (Arnold, 1997) and said, "This book is very silly! It is about a boy and crazy things are happening to his body. As you listen to the story, I want you to see if you can identify the different types of ending punctuation the author uses." Kasey began reading the book. Kasey stopped after the first few pages to point out sentences containing each type of ending punctuation. She read the sentences again for students in order for them to understand how ending punctuation affects the way you read the sentence. She read some of the sentences and changed the punctuation and explained how the reader would interpret it differently if the ending punctuation was different. She read the sentence "It was my stuffing coming out!" (n.p.) and said "This sentence has an exclamation point to convey that the character is shrieking in fright. If the sentence ended in a period, the message would not be interpreted by the reader in the same way." Kasey continued reading and stopped after reading the sentence, "The glue that holds our parts together isn't holding me!!!" (n.p.) and asked students, "Why do you think the author used three exclamation points here?" A student raised his hand and said, "Look at his eyes, his pupils are really small and his eyes are really big!" Kasey replied, "Yes! Look at his face, he is very concerned. He is panicking because he thinks that he is falling apart!" Kasey read the sentence with a monotone voice as if there were a period at the end of the sentence and then again with three exclamation points at the end of the sentence for students to see the effect that punctuation has on the sentence. Emma raised her hand and said, "Look, there's another 9 in the sentence and pointed to the word "isn't." Emma was reminded of the comma that we talked about previously. Kasey replied, "That is something called an apostrophe. An apostrophe is used when we combine two words together to make one word, a contraction. When we take the words "is" and "not" and put them together, we make the word "isn't" which means the same thing as is not. This is something that you will learn more about in a few years, great thinking!" Kasey went on to finish reading the rest of the story as the students laughed at each page. After reading the story, Kasey used Figure 4.2 to reflect on the different sentences from the story and why the author used each type of punctuation.

Students were already very familiar with adding periods at the end of sentences. However, now they had a better understanding of how and why periods are used, as well as how and why to use question marks and exclamation points. Kasey pulled up a document on the board to review each type of ending punctuation by creating examples. She started by saying "Periods are used for statements. We use a period when we want to say something clear and straight to the point like, 'I have a cat.'" Kasey wrote the sentence in the box next to "Period." Then she explained that question marks are used when we ask a question like, "Do you have a cat?" Kasey recorded the sentence. "Finally, exclamation points are used when we want to show expression or an emotion like in the sentence, 'My cat ran away!' I used an exclamation point here to show that I am worried and concerned about my cat." Kasey cleared the board and did another example, but this time asked for students to share an example of each type of punctuation. She recorded the sentences on the board. Students shared sentences about a dog, including "I love my dog." "Is your dog trained?" "My dog ran away!" Kasey said, "Notice how we used the same topic for each sentence, they are all about a cat or a dog. Now it's your turn! I want you to take what you have learned about ending punctuation and create three sentences representing the different types of punctuation." Kasey passed out a paper to each student and said, "Point to the first box with the period. Write a sentence that ends with a period." As students wrote their sentences, Kasey walked around the room and read examples as students finished: "I love my dog." "I went to the park." "I love my mom." "I can ride my bike." Then she said, "Now, point to the next box that has a question mark. Create a sentence on the same topic as your first sentence but this time you are going to ask a question." Kasey continued to walk around the room and support any students who needed help and shared a few more examples as students finished: "Why is there a seed in the apple?" "Is it time for lunch?" "How old are you?" "Is it your birthday?" "Wow, great thinking friends!" Finally, she said, "Point to the last box with the exclamation point. This time you are going to create a sentence with an exclamation point that has an expression: excitement, fear, surprise, worry." Students created their last sentences and then Kasey shared a few examples. "I lost my earring!" "My bike tire is flat!"

"Happy Birthday, Harper!" "Your horse is fast!" When students were finished, she said, "Today we learned about punctuation. We learned about the three types of ending punctuation and then listened to a story to see how and why authors use them. We reviewed some of the examples from the story and then worked together to create some examples. Then, you took what you learned to create your own sentences using the three types of ending punctuation. I am so impressed with your sentences and I appreciate your excitement and enthusiasm you showed during the lesson today, kiss your brains!"

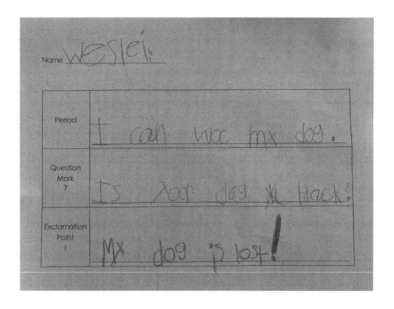

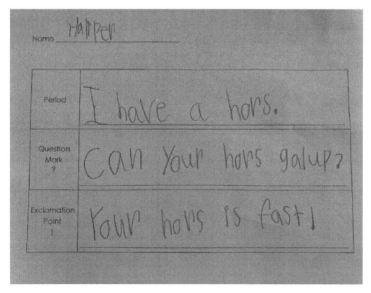

Recommendations for Teaching Students About End Punctuation

Now, let's take a look at an instructional process designed to help early elementary school teachers teach their students about the end punctuation marks of periods, question marks, and exclamation points. The goal of this process is for students to understand what these end punctuation marks are, why they are important to effective writing, and how to use them on their own. The five steps of this sequence are:

1. Introduce the three forms of end punctuation to students.
2. Show students published examples of end punctuation.
3. Discuss the importance of end punctuation to the published examples.
4. Provide students with support as they use end punctuation in sentences.
5. Help students reflect on the importance of carefully selected end punctuation to effective writing.

By engaging students in these instructional steps, you will help them develop a strong foundation of the forms of end punctuation and will support them as they think in careful and reflective ways about how end punctuation is an important and purposefully used tool for effective writing. We'll now explore each part of this process in more specificity.

Step One: Introduce the Three Forms of End Punctuation to Students

This initial instructional step provides students with foundational information about the three forms of end punctuation—periods, question marks, and exclamation points. To introduce these concepts to students, we recommend conducting a mini-lesson that identifies these forms of end punctuation, shares examples of them, and provides introductory information about why writers use them. We encourage you to draw from the examples and explanations in Figure 4.1 in this mini-lesson to give students fundamental insights regarding these concepts. During this lesson, we recommend listing these punctuation forms and their key features on a piece of chart paper and hanging that paper on the wall for students to use as a resource while they write. As you create and hang this chart paper, we encourage you to talk to students about why you're doing this. For example, you might say "I've written down some important ideas about periods, question marks, and exclamation points on this big piece of paper. I'm going to hang it on the wall. The reason I'm doing this is so that you can look at this paper anytime to help you remember these punctuation marks and how to use them."

As you introduce this information to students, we recommend connecting it to previous grammatical concepts the students have worked with—especially the topic of complete sentences discussed in Chapter 3. Doing this will help contextualize end punctuation and will provide a point of reference for students. For example, you might share an explanation such as "Remember how we talked about complete sentences and what makes a sentence complete? One of the important parts of complete sentences that we talked about was end punctuation. That's exactly what we're exploring today! These kinds of end punctuation—periods, question marks, and exclamation points—are the ways we finish complete sentences when we write." This connection to recently studied material can help new concepts such as end punctuation feel more accessible to students. By combining these connections with important fundamental information about punctuation types, you'll give students an excellent foundation that will begin their exploration of this concept and support them throughout this instructional process.

Step Two: Show Students Published Examples of End Punctuation

Now that you've introduced students to fundamental components of end punctuation, the next step is to share with them how these concepts are used in authentic situations. To do this, we recommend conducting a read aloud from a published book that uses each of these end punctuation forms (and visually displaying the book's pages while you read if possible). As you read the book, we encourage you to identify examples of sentences that end with each of these forms of end punctuation and write an example of each type on a piece of chart paper. Doing this will call students' attention to these examples of end punctuation and develop their awareness of the ways these concepts are used in authentic contexts. For example, if you read the book *Beautifully Me* (Noor & Ali, 2021) you can point out the following sentences, each of which concludes with a different type of end punctuation:

"Yesterday, I woke up before the sun."

(n.p.)

"It was my first day of school!"

(n.p.)

"Why was Amma so sad?"

(n.p.)

By identifying sentences concluding with each of these forms of end punctuation, you'll show students how a published author uses periods, exclamation points, and question marks in authentic ways. After you've identified each of these examples, we encourage you to continue to read the book and ask students to identify end punctuation as they follow along. For instance, after you finish each page of the book, you can ask for student volunteers to identify forms of end punctuation they've noticed in the text. Engaging students in this identification of examples of end punctuation can help develop their awareness of the ways these punctuation forms are used in published writing. Once you've finished the book and you feel that students have seen authentic uses of each of these punctuation forms, it's time to move to the next step of the process, which focuses on the importance of end punctuation to the published examples.

Step Three: Discuss the Importance of End Punctuation to the Published Examples

This instructional step extends naturally from the previous activity: after students have seen authentic, published examples of sentences containing periods, question marks, and exclamation points, they are ready to start thinking about why these forms of end punctuation are important to the effectiveness of the sentences in which they're used. To conduct this discussion with students, we recommend returning to a published example of each form of end punctuation that you identified in the previous activity. For each one, we encourage you to talk with your students about the reason the author used the particular example of end punctuation and how the sentence would be different if the author had used a different form of end punctuation instead. For instance, if you were talking to students about the sentence "It was my first day of school!" (n.p.) from *Beautifully Me* (Noor & Ali, 2021) identified in the previous recommendation, you would highlight that the author used the exclamation point to indicate the speaker's excitement about the first day of school. You could then continue to explain that the sentence would be very different if the author had written the sentence with a different punctuation mark. A period would express the information without extra emotion or enthusiasm, and a question mark would make it look like the character was asking a question or expressing confusion about the first day of school.

To guide these discussions, we recommend using the graphic organizer depicted in Figure 4.2 to document the sentences and the corresponding conversations about them. The organizer contains space for the sentence, thoughts on why the author used the end punctuation in that sentence, and ideas regarding how the sentence would be different if other end punctuation

Published Sentence	Why the Author Used the End Punctuation in the Sentence	How the Sentence Would Be Different if Other End Punctuation Was Used

Figure 4.2 End Punctuation Discussion Graphic Organizer

was used. (A reproducible version of this graphic organizer can be found in Appendix B.)

This graphic organizer will help you and your students talk about the impact of the end punctuation on the published sentences you've identified. During this discussion, we encourage you to think aloud your ideas about the first sentence and then gradually ask for increased student participation as you continue to discuss the sentences. This think aloud will provide students with a clear model for what this analysis can look like, which can increase their understanding of the activity and its expectations. While you and your students share insights on the sentences, we recommend writing the ideas on the graphic organizer and projecting an image of it to the front of the room to provide a visual representation of the insights being shared.

Step Four: Provide Students With Support as They Use End Punctuation in Sentences

This component of the instructional process transitions from the end-punctuation-related explanations, identifications, and discussions in the first three steps and toward students' use of end punctuation in writing. To engage students in their use of end punctuation, we recommend setting up stations around the classroom, with each station focused on one form of end punctuation. Before students begin their station work, we suggest explaining to them that they now have the opportunity to create examples of end punctuation. For instance, you might call students' attention to the pieces of chart paper that you've created throughout this instructional process and say "We've been doing great work on end punctuation lately! We've discussed periods, question marks, and exclamations points and have looked at and talked about published examples of them. Today, we'll work in stations to create our own!"

At each station, students will create a sentence that uses the focal form of end punctuation. They can construct these sentences in a variety of ways depending on their individual levels of comfort with the concept and with writing in general. For instance, students can write a sentence, write a sentence and draw a corresponding picture, draw a picture and verbally explain to you what the corresponding sentence would be and what end punctuation would be present, or verbally dictate a sentence and its end punctuation that you or another adult in the room writes down. As students work at each station, we recommend circulating so that you can hold one-on-one conferences with them and provide them with individualized support. During these conferences, you can work with students by helping them choose writing opportunities that align with their comfort levels and by asking them questions about the sentences they are creating and the end punctuation present in the sentence. For example, when meeting with students who are working on using exclamation points, you can talk with them about why an exclamation point would align with their sentence and how their sentence would be different if they didn't use this type of end punctuation. If students seem to be confused about the purpose or impact of the end punctuation with which they're working, you can use that opportunity to provide them with one-on-one instruction. After students have finished their station activities, volunteers can share sentences they created and the end punctuation they used in those sentences.

Step Five: Help Students Reflect on the Importance of Carefully Selected End Punctuation to Effective Writing

Now that students have constructed sentences with purposefully constructed end punctuation, we encourage you to ask them to reflect on the importance of this concept to effective writing. To introduce this reflection, we recommend explaining to students that they'll be building off of the work they did in the last step of the process. For instance, you can compliment students on the work they did creating sentences containing these forms of end punctuation and share the reflection questions they'll be thinking about. Two reflection questions that can guide students' thinking are "Why is it important for writers to think carefully about end punctuation?" and "What do you think would happen if writers didn't pay attention to the end punctuation they use?" These two questions approach the concept of end punctuation from a writerly perspective—in other words, students are asked to think about this topic from the point of view of a writer. Framing the questions this way is important because it asks students to consider the concept of end punctuation as something writers think about when they work.

We recommend presenting each question on a projector screen or piece of chart paper and then asking students to share their responses verbally to each one. As they share their insights, we suggest writing their answers on the projector screen or chart paper on which you displayed the question.

This will help students engage with and learn from each other's insights, which can ultimately encourage increased participation: as students see their peers' ideas, they may then be inspired to share their own reflections. Once a number of students have shared, you can summarize key themes from their responses and this summary to conclude the instructional process in a meaningful and intentional way.

Final Thoughts on End Punctuation

In this final section, we share key points from this chapter, such as essential information about end punctuation, why it is important to effective writing, and recommended instructional practices for teaching early elementary students about this writing tool:

- ◆ The three forms of end punctuation are:
  - – Periods (.)
  - – Question marks (?)
  - – Exclamation points (!)

- ◆ These forms of end punctuation are important to effective writing because they guide readers' understanding of the information in a sentence.
- ◆ When writers decide whether to conclude a sentence with a period, a question mark, or an exclamation point, they are communicating to readers how to read and interpret that sentence.

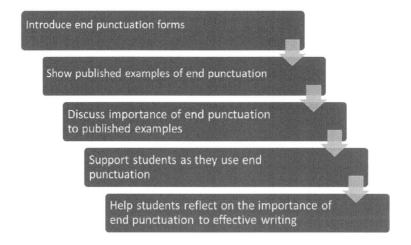

Figure 4.3 End Punctuation Instructional Flowchart

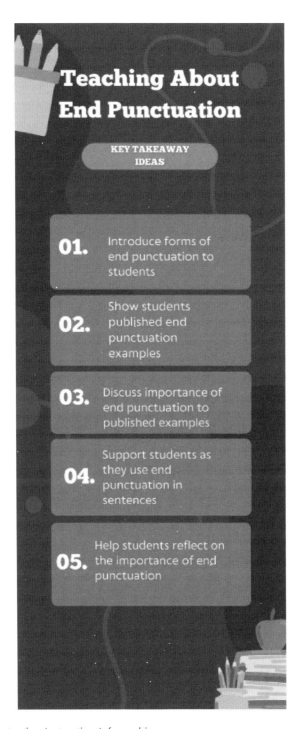

Figure 4.4 End Punctuation Instruction Infographic

This infographic provides an accessible visual representation of a mentor-text-based instruction-al process to use when teaching students about end punctuation. The instructional process it depicts states that teachers should introduce forms of end punctuation to students, show students published end punctuation examples, support students as they use end punctuation in sentences, and help students reflect on the importance of end punctuation. This image is also available on the book's website as downloadable Support Material.

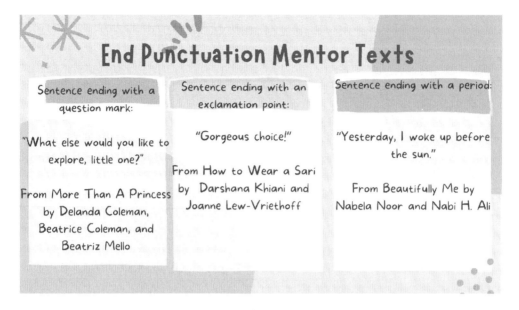

Figure 4.5 End Punctuation Mentor Text Infographic

◆ When teaching early elementary students about end punctuation, we recommend using this instructional process:
  – Introduce the three forms of end punctuation to students.
  – Show students published examples of end punctuation.
  – Discuss the importance of end punctuation to the published examples.
  – Provide students with support as they use end punctuation in sentences.
  – Help students reflect on the importance of carefully selected end punctuation to effective writing.

Figure 4.3 depicts this process in any easy-to-follow flowchart.

This infographic provides a visual representation of key end punctuation mentor texts discussed in this chapter. It features examples of each of the end punctuation forms discussed in the chapter.

5 ⚒

A Big Strategy

The Power of Capitalization

What Is Capitalization?

In this chapter, we'll look closely at an important grammatical concept for clear and effective writing: capitalization. We define capitalization as the use of uppercase letters in ways that correspond with writing conventions. While there are a number of rules about capital letters, this chapter focuses on some major ones that are likely to be relevant to the needs of early elementary school writers:

- ◆ Capitalize the first letter of the first word in a sentence.
- ◆ Capitalize the pronoun I.
- ◆ Capitalize proper nouns—specific names of people, places, and things.
- ◆ Capitalize days of the week, months of the year, and holidays.

By learning about these capitalization concepts, students develop key understandings of how and why words in the English language are capitalized. Figure 5.1 provides examples of each of these four capitalization ideas.

Why Capitalization Is Important to Effective Writing

The grammatical concept of capitalization is a key component of strong writing: by effectively using capitalization in their works, writers can help readers

DOI: 10.4324/9781003302209-6

Concepts	Example
Capitalize the first letter of the first word in a sentence.	**We** are going outside.
Capitalize the pronoun I.	After lunch, **I** will play soccer.
Capitalize proper nouns—specific names of people, places, and things.	Have you been to the **Pacific Ocean**?
Capitalize days of the week, months of the year, and holidays.	We learned that **Thanksgiving** takes place in **November.**

Figure 5.1 Key Capitalization Concepts and Examples

easily understand the information they express. A piece of writing that did not contain any capitalization would be much harder to understand and would likely confuse the reader. For example, if the first letter in a sentence wasn't capitalized, readers might wonder if the sentence actually began at that point or if there was other text that they missed. Similarly, if the name of a proper noun was written without capitalization, readers could be confused regarding whether or not that word is actually a proper noun.

To illustrate the importance of capitalization to strong writing, let's take a look at some published sentences from books written for young readers and reflect on the impact of effective capitalization use on those works. In the book *The Very Hungry Caterpillar* (Carle, 1969), author Eric Carle capitalized the first letters of the words "On" and "Monday" in the sentence "On Monday he ate through one apple" (n.p.). The capitalization of these words is important to the effectiveness of the sentence because of the clarity it provides. By capitalizing "On," Carle clarifies for the reader that this word marks the beginning of a new sentence. Similarly, by capitalizing the first letter of "Monday," Carle ensures that the reader knows that he is referring to a specific day of the week. If these words were not capitalized, readers would likely be confused about the information in the sentence and may focus more on making sense of the information than on enjoying the story. For instance, if Carle wrote "on monday he ate through one apple," readers might wonder if the sentence was intended to begin with the word "on" and if "monday" refers to a day of the week or to something else. The capitalization that Carle uses helps readers understand the caterpillar's experiences.

Another effective use of capitalization to enhance the clarity of a piece is found in the book *Fatima's Great Outdoors* (Tariq & Lewis, 2021). In the sentence "The trip felt like Fatima's reward after a long, hard week" (n.p.), author Ambreen Tariq uses capitalization to ensure that readers comprehend the sentence in the way it was intended. The capitalized first letter of the word "The" at the beginning of the sentence communicates to readers that a new sentence begins with this word; without it, readers might wonder if the author intended to start a sentence in that spot. Also very important to the sentence is the capitalization of the first letter of the word "Fatima": by capitalizing the beginning of this word, Tariq clearly communicates that this word is the name of a specific person. Since Fatima is also the main character of the story, it is especially important that readers identify her name in the sentence as the name of a specific individual—the capitalization helps make this possible.

These examples from *The Very Hungry Caterpillar* and *Fatima's Great Outdoors* show the importance of capitalization to effective writing: by capitalizing the first letters of specific words, the authors of the books help readers understand the information in the ways the authors intended. Now, let's take a look inside Kasey's classroom and see how she helps her students understand the concept of capitalization.

Classroom Snapshot

Kasey began the lesson by asking students, "What do you put at the beginning of a sentence?" Students quickly shouted, "Uppercase letter!" and "Capital letter!" Kasey replied, "Yes, that's right. Very good! Good writers begin sentences with an uppercase letter. The first letter of the first word in a sentence is always capitalized. You all have been working very hard on including this in your writing. However, there are other times that it is important to include capitalization in our writing. Today we are going to learn about capitalization and the rules for capitalization, when we need to use a capital letter." Kasey used Figure 5.1 to introduce the key capitalization concepts and examples. With such a strong focus on letter recognition in kindergarten, Kasey emphasized understanding the capitalizing of "I" by saying, "Remember, 'I' is a letter but it is also a word. When 'I' is by itself, it is a word and it's always a capital letter."

Kasey showed the students the cover of *The Very Hungry Caterpillar* (Carle, 1969) and said, "As you know, this is one of my favorite books and I know all of us have read it many times. Today, our focus is on capitalization. As you listen to this book, I want you to see if you can identify words that are capitalized." Kasey began reading and the students quickly started to recite, "But he was still hungry." after each day. She stopped after Wednesday and said, "Notice the beginning of the sentence starts with an uppercase letter in the word 'On' and 'Wednesday' is a day of the week, so we capitalize the 'W.'" Kasey continued reading the rest of the story. After reading, she directed students' attention to the board and showed them Figure 5.2. She asked, "What words did you identify that were capitalized?" Molly raised her hand and said, "The days of the week!" Kasey replied, "That's right, Molly! Days of the week are capitalized. In this story, we saw all of the days of the week." Kasey wrote the days of the week in the chart and noted the reason for capitalization. Another student raised their hand and said, "The beginning of the sentence had a capital letter." Kasey replied, "Yes, very good! The author used capital letters at the beginning of each sentence in order for us, the readers, to understand where new sentences begin. If the author didn't use capital letters at the beginning of each sentence or a period at the end of each sentence, it would be one long sentence and it would be hard for readers to understand the story." Kasey referred back to the book with students and they identified some of the first words in the beginning of sentences, "In, One, On, Now." Kasey recorded these on the chart and noted the reason for capitalization was the beginning of a sentence.

Kasey explained, "In the story we read today, we saw examples of how capital letters are used for the beginning of a sentence and days of the week." She pulled up Figure 5.1 on the board and directed students' attention back to the board to review the concepts for capitalization again. Then she said, "Now that we know and understand the different concepts, or rules, for capitalization in writing, it is time to practice them in our own writing. You are going to write a sentence including one or more of the rules for capitalization." Kasey showed the students the Student Assessment Graphic Organizer and said, "This is the paper that we are going to use to work on our writing. I want you to write your sentence in this box (Kasey drew an arrow pointing to the box with "Use the example in a sentence") and draw a picture to match your sentence in this box (Kasey drew a star next to the box with "Draw a picture of what's happening in the sentence"). I will help you with the other parts. Go ahead and get started and I will be coming around to help you." Students began writing their sentences and drawing pictures. Kasey went around the room and individually talked with students about their sentences. She asked Kaelin to read her sentence. Kaelin read, "My friend has a party on Memorial Day." Kasey said, "Very good! Can you identify where you included capital letters?" Kaelin pointed to her sentence and said, "The 'M' in 'My' because it is the beginning of my sentence and the 'M' and 'D' in 'Memorial Day' because it is a holiday." Kasey replied, "That's right, excellent!" Kasey recorded the "Concept" and "Example" on Kaelin's paper and said, "The concept we are focusing on is 'Capitalization' and the example you used is a 'Holiday.'" At this time, Kasey did not focus on the "Why the example of the concept is important to the sentence:" box on the template since she orally discussed concepts with students. Kasey continued to work with a few other students and then shared some of the examples with the class. Kasey ended the lesson by saying, "Today we learned about capitalization. We learned the different concepts, or rules, for capitalization and looked at examples of each one. Then we listened to a story to see how an author uses capitalization in his writing. After reading, we reviewed the rules of capitalization again and then you had a chance to apply what you learned into your own writing. As you continue to work on your writing, remember to include capitalization in your sentences."

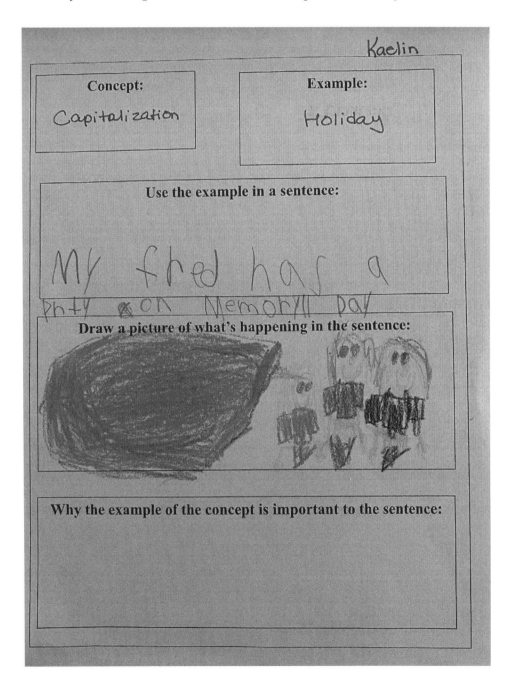

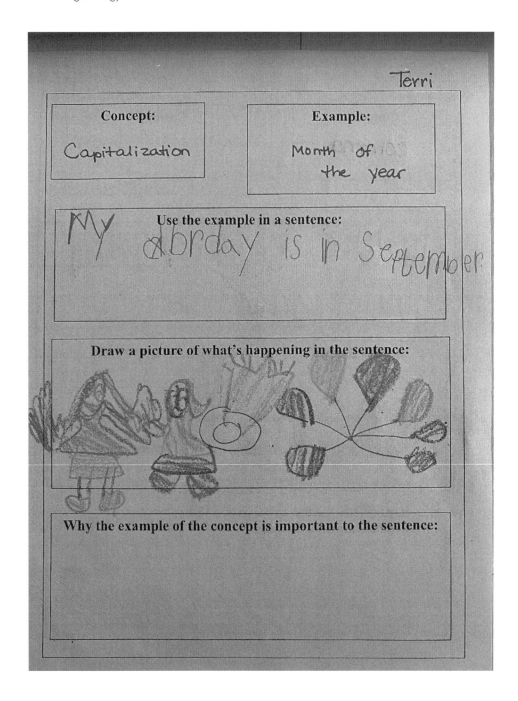

Concept:	Example:
Capitalization	Month of the year

Use the example in a sentence:

My abrday is in September

Draw a picture of what's happening in the sentence:

Why the example of the concept is important to the sentence:

Terri

Recommendations for Teaching Students About Capitalization

In this section, we share a step-by-step instructional process to use when helping your students understand capitalization. These instructional steps use a combination of explanation, discussion, and application to help students understand key capitalization concepts, why these concepts are important, and how to implement the concepts in their own writing. This procedure consists of five key components:

1. Introduce important capitalization concepts to students.
2. Show students published examples of these capitalization concepts.
3. Talk with students about the reasons specific words are capitalized.
4. Work with students as they apply these capitalization concepts to their own pieces.
5. Help students reflect on the importance of capitalization to effective writing.

This instructional process privileges mentor text use, application, and reflection, using these components to help students understand why capitalization is an important tool that writers use to make their works as effective as possible. Let's now look at each of the steps in more detail.

Step One: Introduce Important Capitalization Concepts to Students

To prepare students for the work they'll do with capitalization in this instructional sequence, we recommend establishing a knowledge foundation by introducing important capitalization ideas. To begin building this base of understanding, we recommend conducting brief, focused mini-lessons associated with each of the capitalization concepts described in the opening section of this chapter and in Figure 5.1. In each mini-lesson, we recommend introducing the relevant capitalization-related idea to students, sharing an example of it, and providing any elaboration and explanation you feel might help students understand it. For example, as you talk with students about the capitalization concept "Capitalize the first letter of the first word in a sentence," you can share with them the example "We are going outside" found in Figure 5.1. As you talk with students about this information, we encourage you to write the capitalization concepts and examples on a piece of chart paper and post those papers in easy-to-see places around the classroom. These posted examples will provide students with visual reminders of these concepts, to which they can refer throughout this instructional process and in their future writing activities.

When introducing these capitalization concepts, it's important to emphasize to students that they're not expected to memorize all of this information immediately. You might explain that the class is going to be working together to explore the idea of capitalization and some of the reasons writers capitalize certain special words in their works. While sharing these introductory points, you could also preview the rest of the instructional process for students, explaining that they're going to start by looking at some reasons why we capitalize certain special words when we write and then sharing that the class is going to look at some published books and the capitalized words in them. You can then tell students that after they look at these published examples, they'll work on creating their own examples of capitalized words. During this explanation, we recommend referring back to the posted examples of capitalization concepts and explaining that students can use them, with a statement such as "These examples we just talked about are here on our classroom wall and will stay there. If you need a reminder about capitalization, just look over here and check them out."

Step Two: Show Students Published Examples of These Capitalization Concepts

Now that students are familiar with key capitalization information, we recommend further engaging them in the topic by showing them published examples of these concepts. We suggest doing this by conducting read alouds from engaging picture books that include words that are capitalized for a range of reasons. (This range of capitalization reasons is important so that you can show students a variety of capitalization concepts in the text.) As you read the book—and display it, if possible, on a projector screen using a document camera—we encourage you to call students' attention to a variety of capitalized words in the piece. For instance, the following excerpt from *Flossie and the Fox* (McKissack & Isadora, 1986) contains examples of all four of the capitalization types discussed in this chapter: "'Here I am, Big Mama,' Flossie said after catching her breath. It was hot, hotter than a usual Tennessee August day" (n.p). As you read this passage to your students and display the text for them, you can identify each of these capitalized words. Then, as you keep reading the book, you can ask for student volunteers to raise their hands and identify other words that begin with capital letters. For example, after you read aloud a page and students follow along, they can share examples of capitalization that stand out to them. This identification will further develop students' awareness of this concept and show them that capitalization is frequently used in published texts. In addition, it will prepare students well for the next step of this process, when they'll think about the reasons specific words in these published examples are capitalized.

Step Three: Talk With Students About the Reasons Specific Words Are Capitalized

This instructional step further develops students' knowledge of capitalization by engaging them in discussions and activities focused on why the published examples shared in the previous step are capitalized. To maximize students' success on this activity, we recommend first reviewing the capitalization concepts you discussed with them in the first step of this process. To do this, you can return to the chart paper you created during those initial mini-lessons and remind students of each of these reasons that authors capitalize words when they write. After you review this information, we suggest transitioning to the connection between these concepts and published examples. For example, you might tell students, "Now that we've reviewed why authors capitalize words, we're going to connect this knowledge to the published examples of capitalization we just read together. We're going to look at some of these published examples of capitalization and talk together about why those words were capitalized."

Once you've introduced this work to students, we suggest selecting a passage from the book you read during step two of this process that contains several capitalized words. The activity is most effective if those words are capitalized for a variety of reasons—this will provide opportunities to discuss a range of capitalization concepts and look at their authentic uses. After you revisit this passage with students, we encourage you to create a chart on which to record capitalized words in the passage and the reasons they're capitalized. (An example of such a chart is depicted in Figure 5.2 and also available in Appendix B.)

Capitalized Word	Reason It Is Capitalized

Figure 5.2 Capitalization Graphic Organizer

For example, if you use the excerpt from *Flossie and the Fox* (McKissack & Isadora, 1986) described earlier in the chapter that reads " 'Here I am, Big Mama,' Flossie said after catching her breath. It was hot, hotter than a usual Tennessee August day" (n.p), you can then work with students to identify capitalized words in the passage and the reasons they're capitalized. For instance, the word "Here" would be accompanied by the explanation "First word in the sentence," "Big Mama" would be paired with an explanation such as "Proper noun—a person's name," and "Tennessee" would be explained as "Proper noun—a state's name." We recommend completing this chart with students by gradually releasing responsibility and ownership. For example, you can first identify some capitalized words in the text and think aloud about why those words are capitalized. As the activity continues, you can ask students to share their thoughts on which capitalization concept each capitalized word represents. This can further engage students in the activity and develop their understanding of this writing tool.

Step Four: Work With Students as They Apply These Capitalization Concepts to Their Own Pieces

Now that students have thought carefully about the reasons published words are capitalized, it's time for them to take even more ownership over their work with this concept by applying the capitalization concepts to pieces they create. To do this, we recommend asking students to work on pieces of writing that contain words that are capitalized for a variety of reasons. For example, a piece might contain words whose first letters are capitalized because they begin sentences, because they identify specific people, and because they name particular months of the year. Before students begin to create these compositions, we encourage you to remind them of the capitalization concepts they've explored and to highlight the published examples with which they recently engaged. To do this, you can conduct a review mini-lesson that reminds students of the reasons authors use capitalization, making connections to the chart paper you created in the first instructional step and the published examples examined in steps two and three.

After this review discussion, we suggest telling students that it's now their time to be authors who use capitalization in their works. To put students in this active role, we recommend that each student takes on the responsibility of creating a sentence that contains at least two capitalized words. Depending on where students are in their writing and literacy levels, they can compose these sentences in different ways, such as writing their own sentence and capitalizing the relevant words, dictating the text to the teacher and identifying which words should be capitalized, or drawing a picture and verbally sharing what is taking place and which words should be capitalized in the description. While students work on creating these sentences, we encourage you to confer with them individually, talking with them about the capitalized words in their sentences. In these conferences, we recommend asking the students to tell you the reason associated with each capitalized word in their sentence. For example, if a student capitalized an individual's name, you can talk with them about the choice to make sure that they know why they capitalized the word. These conferences are also useful times to correct possible misunderstandings: if a student capitalized a word that didn't need to be capitalized or did not capitalize a word that should be, you can review the capitalization concepts discussed earlier in the process to help them understand the information and apply it to their writing.

Step Five: Help Students Reflect on the Importance of Capitalization to Effective Writing

We recommend concluding this instructional process by supporting students as they reflect on the importance of capitalization to effective writing. Engaging in reflection about the significance of this grammatical concept to effective writing can help students think about capitalization as a tool for effective writing that authors use to maximize the strength of their works. To help students reflect on this concept, we recommend asking them questions such as "Why do you think it's important that authors use capitalization when they write?" and "What would it be like to read a piece of writing that didn't have any capitalization?" As students respond to these questions, you can help them consider the ways that capitalization helps readers understand what they're reading. Capitalization, for example, helps readers identify when a sentence begins, when an author refers to a specific person, place, or thing, and when the author refers to a particular day of the week or month of the year. By asking students to think about the effect that capitalization has on a piece of writing and how different a text would be without this concept, we can help them think in metacognitive ways about the importance of this grammatical tool. Through this reflection, students' perceptions on capitalization can shift from something we're told to do when we write to a strategy that authors use to make their works clear and to ensure that readers understand the ideas in the ways the author intended.

Final Thoughts on Capitalization

In this section, we discuss key information from this chapter, including central concepts about capitalization, why this tool is important to effective writing, and recommendations for teaching early elementary school students about capitalization:

◆ We define capitalization as the use of uppercase letters in ways that correspond with writing conventions.
◆ Some major capitalization concepts likely to be relevant to the needs of early elementary school writers are:
  – Capitalize the first letter of the first word in a sentence.
  – Capitalize the pronoun I.
  – Capitalize proper nouns—specific names of people, places, and things.
  – Capitalize days of the week, months of the year, and holidays.

◆ Capitalization is an important tool for effective writing—by capitalizing the first letters of specific words, the authors help readers understand information in the ways they intended.
◆ If authors did not use capitalization, readers would likely be confused about the information in the text and may focus more on making sense of the information than on enjoying the piece.
◆ When teaching early elementary students about the concept of capitalization, we recommend following this instructional process:

  – Introduce important capitalization concepts to students.
  – Show students published examples of these capitalization concepts.

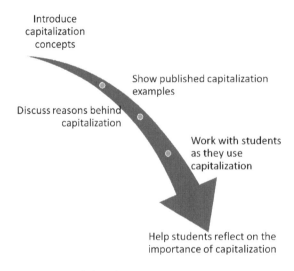

Figure 5.3 Capitalization Instructional Flowchart

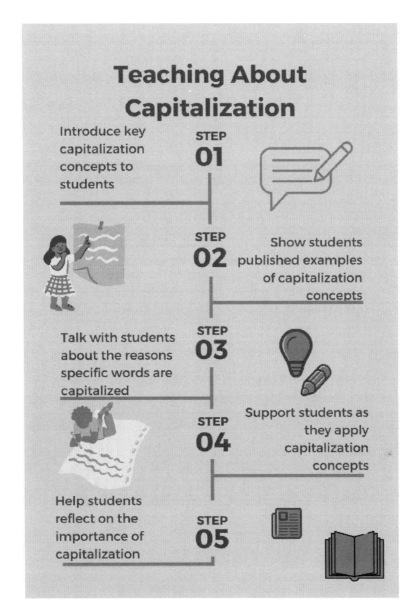

Figure 5.4 Capitalization Instruction Infographic

This infographic provides a visual representation of a mentor-text-based instructional process to use when teaching students about capitalization. It explains that, in effective capitalization instruction, teachers should introduce key capitalization concepts to students, show students published examples of capitalization concepts, talk with students about the reasons specific words are capitalized, support students as they apply capitalization concepts, and help students reflect on the importance of capitalization. This image is also available on the book's website as downloadable Support Material.

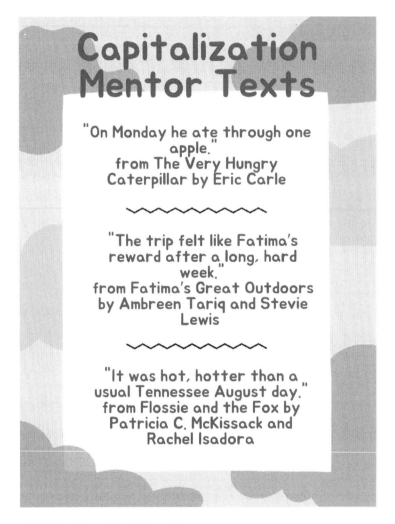

Figure 5.5 Capitalization Mentor Text Infographic

- – Talk with students about the reasons specific words are capitalized.
- – Work with students as they apply these capitalization concepts to their own pieces.
- – Help students reflect on the importance of capitalization to effective writing.

Figure 5.3 depicts this process in an easy-to-follow flowchart.

This infographic displays key capitalization mentor texts discussed in this chapter.

6

Question Time

Why and How Do Writers Use Question Words?

What Are Question Words?

Think about a time when you've asked a question. You might have said something like, "What do you want to eat for dinner?," "When does the game start?," "Who is coming to the party?," or another similarly constructed sentence. Each of these sentences begins with a word that indicates what kind of information the speaker is trying to learn, such as "what," "when," or "who." In this chapter, we'll call these kinds of words "question words" because they play important roles in the process of asking a question and often introduce those questions. Figure 6.1 lists the question words that we'll explore in this chapter and provides examples of each of them used in sentences.

It's important to know that each of these question words has a specific meaning and is used to ask for a certain type of information. For example, "where" is used to ask a question about a location (such as the example sentence in Figure 6.1, "Where do you want to sit). By comparison, the question word "who" is used for a different purpose—to identify a particular person or group. In the example in Figure 6.1, "Who is going to the movie theater?," the word "who" is used to find out the identity of the person referenced in the question. Figure 6.2 lists each of the question words described in Figure 6.1 and describes the type of information associated with the word.

Now that we've looked at examples and features of question words, let's consider why these words are important tools for effective writing.

DOI: 10.4324/9781003302209-7

Question Word	Example Sentence
Who	Who is going to the movie theater?
What	What movie is playing?
When	When does the movie start?
Where	Where do you want to sit?
Why	Why couldn't she come to the movie with us?
How	How was your trip to the movie theater?

Figure 6.1 Question Words and Examples of Their Use

Question Word	Related Information
Who	"Who" relates to the person or group asked about in a question. We use this word to find out information about a person or group of people.
What	"What" relates to a fact, thing, or object. When we use the question word "what," we're usually trying to find one of these pieces of information.
When	"When" refers to the time of an event. We use this word when we want to know the time that something happened, is happening, or will happen.
Where	"Where" refers to a place, such as the location of an event or an object. When we want to find out information about a location, we use the question word "where."
Why	"Why" relates to a reason that something takes place. We use this word when we want an explanation of an event or a piece of information.
How	"How" relates to the way something was done, such as the example "How was your trip to the movie theater?" in Figure 6.1. In addition, "how" can also relate to an amount, such as "How many hours long is the movie?"

Figure 6.2 Question Words and Related Information

Why Question Words Are Important to Effective Writing

Question words are important tools for effective writing because they clearly indicate to readers that a question is being asked. In addition, the particular question word the author chooses to use lets the reader know the type of information being requested. For instance, when a writer uses the word "who" in a question, it not only shows the reader that a question is being asked, but also makes sure the reader understands that the question being asked relates to a person. By carefully selecting the question word that best aligns with a situation, a writer can craft a question that is easy to understand and asks for relevant and useful information.

In the book *We Walk Through the Forest* (Ferland & Popova, 2020), author Lisa Ferland uses the question word "what" to clearly communicate information in the excerpt "Birds sing, twigs snap, and leaves rustle. What's up ahead?" (n.p.). In this passage, the word "what" is important to the effectiveness of the text: it tells readers about the focus of the question, letting them know that the speaker is asking about some kind of thing or object that might be up ahead in the woods. If Ferland had used a different question word here, readers would interpret the sentence differently. For example, if the passage read "Who is up ahead?," we might picture a person standing in the woods. In addition, if the text read "Where is up ahead?," readers might think that the speaker is trying to find a particular place. By using the word "what," Lisa Ferland communicates to the reader exactly what information the speaker is trying to learn.

Another text that purposefully and effectively uses question words is the book *Above the Rim: How Elgin Baylor Changed Basketball* (Bryant & Morrison, 2020). In the passage "'Where did he learn those moves?' the other players asked," author Jen Bryant uses the word "where" to indicate that the players who asked this question wanted to know information about the specific place where all-time great basketball player Elgin Baylor learned his moves. If Bryant had used another question word instead, the information the other players asked for would be very different. For instance, if the text used the question word "when" to create the passage "'When did he learn those moves?' the other players asked," the players would be wondering about the time that Elgin Baylor learned his basketball moves instead of the place he learned them. Similarly, if Bryant used the word "how" in the question instead of "where," the players would be asking about the way Baylor learned the moves.

These examples from *We Walk Through the Forest* (Ferland & Popova, 2020) and *Above the Rim: How Elgin Baylor Changed Basketball* (Bryant & Morrison, 2020) show the impact of question words on a piece of writing. By using question words in the identified passages from these books, the authors of these texts help their reader understand two pieces of information: 1) a question is being asked, and 2) the kind of information being asked for. Question words are important tools for effective writing because of the way they provide this information. Now, let's look at the classroom snapshot and check out how Kasey helps her students understand this concept.

Classroom Snapshot

Kasey began the lesson by asking students to share examples of questions. She said, "Share with me a question that you have asked before . . . any question." Students raised their hands and shared, "What color is the sky?" "Where is my dog?" "Do you like apples?" "When is it going to be time for lunch?" "Why is it raining?" As students shared questions, Kasey recorded the words "What, Where, When, Why" on an anchor chart. She replied, "When you shared your questions, these are some of the words you used. These are just a few of the words that we use to ask questions." Kasey directed students to the board and used Figure 6.1 to introduce the question words and an example of each. After introducing the question words, she used Figure 6.2 to further explain how each question word is used, the purpose. She read the question word and related information for each one and then gave an example for each, such as " 'Who' refers to a person, like 'Who is your teacher?' ", " 'What' refers to a thing, like 'What color are your eyes?' ", " 'Where' refers to location, like 'Where is my pencil?' or 'Where is your birthday party?' "

Kasey introduced the book *We Walk Through the Forest* (Ferland & Popova, 2020) and said, "Today, we are going to read this book about a girl and her dog who go on an adventure through the forest. As you listen to the story, see if you can identify question words the author uses." Kasey began reading the story and stopped after the first few pages and asked, "What do you notice?" Harper raised her hand and said, "Every page says, 'Do you see what I see?' " Kasey replied, "Yes, that's right. Each time she stops to ask the same question." Kasey continued reading and stopped before the last page and asked, "What do you think Mama sees? Look at the picture and make a prediction, what do you think it is?" Students shared, "A dog!" "A dragon!" "A bird!" Kasey turned the page and read, "We see—not a bear—but a silly old MOOSE!" (n.p.). After reading, Kasey used Figure 6.3 to review the questions from the story. She asked, "What are some of the question words you heard in the story?" Terri raised her hand and shared, "What?" Kasey replied, "Very good, Terri! In the story, the author used the question word

'What' when Mama asked, 'So, what gave you a scare?' " Kasey recorded the word "What" on the graphic organizer and the example and then discussed with the class, "The author used the word "What' when Mama asked the girl about what happened in the forest. So, the girl told her Mama exactly what happened on her adventure and the things she saw." Kasey also reflected on the repetitive use of "Do you see what I see?" and the importance of that question throughout the story.

Kasey directed students back to Figure 6.1 to review the question words and an example of how to use each one. She then revisited the anchor chart from the beginning of the lesson and asked students, "Are there any new question words that we learned that we can add to our chart?" Students raised their hands and shared, "How" and "Why." Then she said, "Now that we understand question words, I want you to create some questions." As part of the ABC End of Year Activities, this day was "Q" for Questions. Kasey connected the lesson to the activity by having students ask questions about first grade. Kasey explained, "Today is 'Q' for questions. You are going to create questions about first grade. What are you wondering about first grade? What do you want to know about first grade? I want you to use these question words (she pointed to the anchor chart) to create your questions." Kasey showed students their writing paper and explained that students are to try to write three questions. She passed out their papers and students began writing. As students worked on their questions, Kasey walked around the room to support students. When students were finished writing, Kasey asked students to share some of the questions they created. Kasey closed the lesson by saying, "Today we learned about question words. We learned about the different question words and how they are used. Then, we listened to a story to identify examples of how an author used question words to tell a story. Finally, you took what you learned and applied it to your writing by creating your own questions. Now that you know and understand the different question words, I challenge you to see if you can use them in conversation when sharing your thoughts and ideas as well as in your writing."

Upon reflecting on the lesson taught, Kasey realized something that would be more helpful in her students' understanding of the question words. When creating an anchor chart, rather than just writing the question words, it would be more beneficial to include visuals for each word. Kasey had directed her students to use the anchor chart when writing their questions, but she had several students ask her, "What word is—?" because some of them couldn't read them. Including visuals would make it easier for students to identify the words independently and they would also be able to refer to the anchor chart later.

Name: Harper

Questions About 1st Grade

1. Wen is lonch?

2. *What is* Wuss the teechers name?

3. Where is the class room?

Name: Kaelin

Questions About 1st Grade

1. Who will be my techr?

Who will we geet to go oot side for resces?

2. When will we have Pe?

What tep of books will we read?

3. What will my techs name.

What will we do in cass?

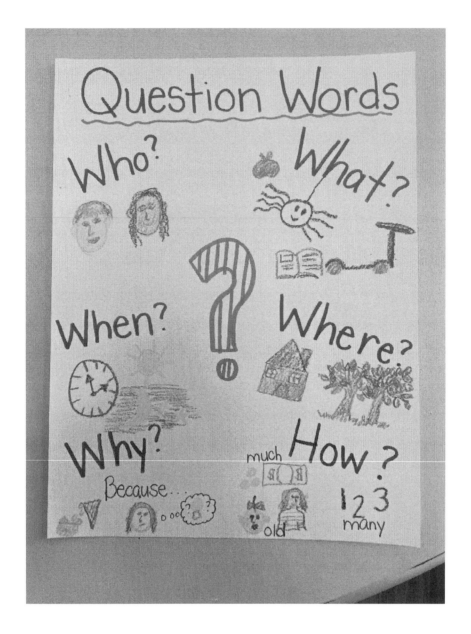

Recommendations for Teaching Students About Question Words

Here, we present a five-step teaching process that we recommend using when teaching early elementary school students about question words. Through this process, students will think carefully about what question words are, why they are important to effective writing, and how to include question words in their own written works. The five steps of this instructional process are:

1. Talk with students about examples of question words and the information associated with them.
2. Show students how published authors use question words in their writing.
3. Discuss with students the question words the authors used and the reasons they used those words.
4. Work with students as they use question words in their writing.
5. Help students reflect on why question words are important writing tools.

By using this instructional process, you'll help students develop strong understandings of this writing tool and give them the skills to reflect on the impact of question words in both the books they read and the pieces of writing they create. Let's now take an in-depth look at the components of this sequence.

Step One: Talk With Students About Examples of Question Words and the Information Associated With Them

This initial step establishes a strong foundation for students by introducing them to what question words are and helping them understand the kind of information connected to those words. The point of this step is to provide students with an accessible point of entry into this concept. As the instructional process continues, students will continue to work with this concept and develop their understanding, so it's not necessary for students to initially memorize the information to which they're introduced here. Instead, we recommend emphasizing to students that they'll be working with the idea of question words throughout the process and that they'll have many opportunities to deepen their knowledge of these words and why they're used.

To begin this process, we recommend activating students' prior knowledge by asking them to think about examples of questions they've asked or that others have asked them. After students share these examples and you provide some of your own, you can then talk with them about the idea of question words with an explanation such as, "A lot of times we use words called question words that are important to the questions we ask. These words show the kinds of information we're asking for in our questions." After sharing these ideas, we recommend calling attention to some of the question words used in the example questions that students provided and the ones that you shared. You might call attention to similarities in the question words that students used (such as several students using the word "who" at the beginning of a question) as well as differences (like other words used in the examples, such as "where," "how," or "why").

After you've introduced the concept of question words to students, we suggest sharing with them the question words depicted in Figure 6.1 and examples of these words used in sentences. We like to put these words and examples on a piece of chart paper and hang up that paper so that students can return to them throughout the process. As you present each question word and example to students, we suggest also discussing the kind of information associated with each word. For instance, if you share with students the sentence "Where do you want to sit?," you can talk with them about how the word "where" refers to a place. After sharing this information regarding each question word, we suggest creating another piece of chart paper that lists each question word and what information it is used to find. (The chart in Figure 6.2 provides explanations of each of these question words that you can use as you do this.) Once you've introduced this information to your students, you will have established a strong foundation related to question words that they can draw on throughout this process.

Step Two: Show Students How Published Authors Use Question Words in Their Writing

This instructional step builds off of the foundation established in the first part of the process: now that students have engaged with some key information related to question words, we can further their learning by showing them how these words look in authentic, published examples. To do this, we recommend reading aloud from a book that is accessible and engaging to your students and projecting the book's pages using a document camera. When you reach question words, we suggest identifying those words and writing them on a piece of chart paper or on the board. For example, if you use the book *What Will I Be?* (Joseph, 2020), you can identify the word "what" in the book's title as an example of a question word. As you continue reading the text, you can also identify the question "How cool is that?" (Joseph, 2020, n.p.) and note that the "how" is a question word in this sentence.

Once you've shown your students a published text containing question words, you can increase their responsibility by asking them to identify question words in another text. For instance, the book *I'm Not a Baby!* (McElmurry, 2006) contains question words such as "where" in the sentence "Where is our baby?" and "who" in "Who ever said he was a baby?" (n.p.). As you read this book (or another one with effectively used question words) with students, you can ask them to identify examples of question words in the text. By identifying examples of these words, students will further develop their familiarity with and understanding of question words in writing.

Step Three: Discuss With Students the Question Words the Authors Used and the Reasons They Used Those Words

Now that students have experience with published versions of question words, they are ready for the next step of this instructional process, which calls for them to think about the reasons the authors of the published texts used the question words they did. Doing this requires students to think not only about the question words that published authors used, but also the information associated with each word. To conduct these discussions with your students, we recommend first returning to the question words you and the students identified in published texts during the previous step. Once you've identified those words, we encourage you to talk with your students about the information associated with each question word and why that information is important to the question being asked. For example, if you discuss the word "where" in the sentence "Where is our baby?" (McElmurry, 2006, n.p.), you can discuss with the students that "where" refers to a location and that the author used this word to show that the character wanted to know the baby's location.

To structure these discussions, we recommend using a chart like the one depicted in Figure 6.3. (A reproducible version of this chart is also available in Appendix B.)

As you complete the chart with students, you'll work with them to note the question word in a particular sentence, identify the information associated

Question Word	Information Associated With It	Why We Think the Author Used This Question Word Here

Figure 6.3 Question Word Discussion Graphic Organizer

with that question word, and reflect on why the author used that particular question word in the piece. For example, if you do this activity with the previously described passage from *Above the Rim: How Elgin Baylor Changed Basketball*, "'Where did he learn those moves?' the other players asked," (Bryant & Morrison, 2020, n.p.), you'd start by identifying "where" as the question word in the sentence. After that, you'd move to the section on the graphic organizer that asks for the information associated with this question word. To complete this section, you could ask students for their thoughts on what kind of information the author is referring to when using the question word "where." In this discussion, you would help students understand and express that this question word is associated with information about a place—in this case, the place where Elgin Baylor learned his moves. Following this, you can help students reflect on why the author may have chosen to use the word "where" in this situation. To do so, we suggest encouraging students to think about the impact and meaning of that specific question word and its alignment with the situation. For instance, you can introduce this reflection by saying, "We've talked about a bunch of different question words that writers can use. Why might the writer have used the question word 'where' in this sentence? Why do you think they picked that word instead of another one?" As students share their thoughts, you can help them think about the fact that the word "where" is the one that is best aligned with the information that the author wants to learn.

Step Four: Work With Students as They Use Question Words in Their Writing

This instructional step provides students with the opportunity to put the knowledge they've developed about question words to use by incorporating these words in written works that they create. To facilitate this work, we recommend asking students to work in ways they feel comfortable to create a sentence that asks a question and uses a question word to help find out information. Depending on students' levels of comfort and familiarity with writing, they could write a sentence on their own, write one with some guidance from the teacher, dictate a sentence to the teacher, or draw a picture associated with a question and verbally express the corresponding question. Before students construct these question sentences, we suggest reminding them of the different question words they've learned about and the information aligned with each word. By reviewing this information, you'll help students think of the purposeful use of question words and create the conditions for them to use these tools in strategic ways in their own writing.

While students work on their sentences, we recommend holding individual conferences with them in which you monitor their work and provide them with support. During these conferences, we encourage you to ask students for three pieces of information: 1) The question word they used, 2) The information they want to learn, 3) Why they chose to use that question word. As you talk with students about this information, you can check on their understanding of the features and effects of the question words they used and do some on-the-spot teaching if students express any confusion. For instance, if you confer with a student who uses the question word "why" in a sentence (such as "Why was school closed yesterday?"), that student would first identify "why" as the question word. Next, you'd talk with the student about what they want to learn from asking this question. (For example, a student asking this question might share that they want to know the reason school was closed the previous day.) After you and the student have discussed these ideas, you can ask them to share why they chose that question word. This conference question is important because it shows the student's understanding of the connection between the question word and the information they want to know. In addition, it emphasizes that specific question words relate to certain pieces of information. In the situation of this example, you can talk with the student to help them be able to express that the question word "why" relates to a reason, such as the reason school was closed. By engaging students in these conference conversations, we can get a good sense of their awareness of the impacts and attributes of question words and guide their understanding in individualized ways.

Step Five: Help Students Reflect on Why Question Words Are Important Writing Tools

We feel that an especially effective way to conclude this instructional process is by creating opportunities for students to reflect on the importance of question words to effective writing. Engaging students in this reflective work can help them further develop their knowledge of the impact of a grammatical concept such as question words and use that understanding to guide them as they implement this writing tool in their future work. Before students reflect, we like to remind them of the great work they've done with this concept and then transition into the reflection activity. For example, you might tell students, "You've done such a great job with question words! You've learned about the question words that writers use, checked out some published examples, discussed those examples, and created some of your own. Nice work! Now, we're going to take some time and reflect on the importance of question words to good writing."

To help students think about why question words are important writing tools, we recommend asking them the following questions: "Why do writers use question words?" and "When you ask a question, why is it important to think about the question word you use?" As they respond to these reflection prompts, students will consider the significance of question words in general, as well as the impact of specific question words that align with particular pieces of information. For instance, a student might respond to the first question by noting that writers use question words to show that a question is being asked. A student could then answer the second question by stating that it's important to think about the specific question word you use because different question words ask for different pieces of information. While your students reflect on these questions, we encourage you to help them think about the importance of question words so that they can further strengthen their understanding of this important concept.

Final Thoughts on Question Words

To conclude this chapter, we present essential ideas about question words, including important information about this concept, why it is important to

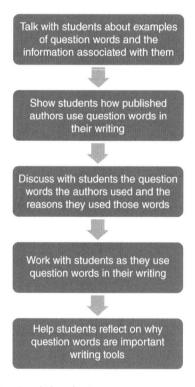

Figure 6.4 Question Word Instructional Flowchart

effective writing, and ideas to consider when teaching early elementary students about question words:

◆ The question words we discuss in this chapter are who, what, when, where, why, and how.
◆ We identify these words as "question words" because they play important roles in the process of asking a question and often introduce those questions.
◆ Each question word relates to a specific type of information. Figure 6.2 in this chapter identifies the information associated with each question word.

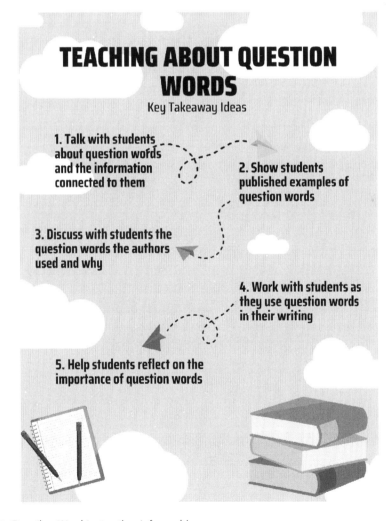

Figure 6.5 Question Word Instruction Infographic

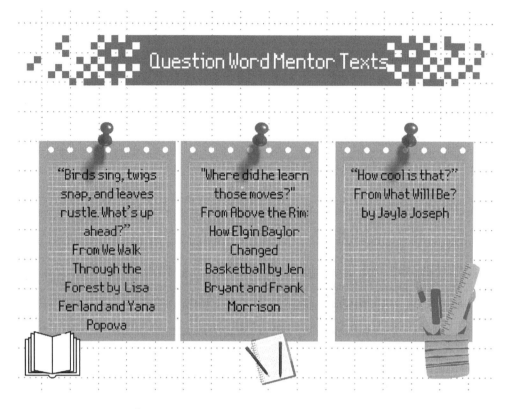

Question Word Mentor Texts

"Birds sing, twigs snap, and leaves rustle. What's up ahead?"
From We Walk Through the Forest by Lisa Ferland and Yana Popova

"Where did he learn those moves?"
From Above the Rim: How Elgin Baylor Changed Basketball by Jen Bryant and Frank Morrison

"How cool is that?"
From What Will I Be? by Jayla Joseph

Figure 6.6 Question Word Mentor Text Infographic

◆ Question words are important tools for effective writing for two key reasons:
  – They clearly indicate to readers that a question is being asked.
  – The particular question word the author chooses to use lets the reader know the type of information being requested.
◆ When teaching early elementary students about question words, we recommend following this instructional process:
  – Talk with students about examples of question words and the information associated with them.
  – Show students how published authors use question words in their writing.
  – Discuss with students the question words the authors used and the reasons they used those words.
  – Work with students as they use question words in their writing.
  – Help students reflect on why question words are important writing tools.

Figure 6.4 depicts this process in an easy-to-follow flowchart.

This infographic provides a visual representation of a mentor-text-based instructional process to use when teaching students about question words.

This infographic displays key question word mentor texts discussed in this chapter.

7

Time to Connect

Using Conjunctions to Create Effective Writing

What Are Conjunctions?

Conjunctions are words that combine ideas or link statements in a piece of writing. While there are a variety of conjunction types with which students will engage throughout their educational careers, in this chapter we focus on key conjunction types that are accessible to early elementary school writers and will help students develop foundational knowledge of this concept. The conjunctions we address in this chapter are the coordinating conjunctions "and," "or," "so," and "but." Something that's very interesting about these conjunctions is that even though they all connect ideas, they all have different meanings and therefore are used in different ways. For example, the conjunction "so" is used to show a connection between two pieces of information, such as in the sentence "The students were hungry, so they had a snack before recess." However, the conjunction "but" is used to indicate a difference or contrast between two things, such as "We waited in line to buy tickets, but the show sold out before we could get them." Figure 7.1 lists each of this chapter's focal conjunctions, describes how each one is used, and provides an example of it used in a sentence.

Now that we've looked at features and examples of these essential conjunctions, let's explore why they are tools for strong writing.

DOI: 10.4324/9781003302209-8

Conjunction	Description of Its Usage	Example of It Used in a Sentence
And	The conjunction "and" is used to show that pieces of information are similar and connected.	"I brought cookies to the party, and my friend brought a cake."
Or	The conjunction "or" shows options, possibilities, and alternatives.	"I could go for a walk, or I could go for a bike ride."
So	The conjunction "so" shows that one piece of information makes another one possible.	"It is hot outside, so we will go to the pool."
But	The conjunction "but" shows that one piece of information is different from another or contrasts with it in some way.	"We scored a lot of points, but our team still lost the game."

Figure 7.1 Key Conjunction Information

Why Conjunctions Are Important to Effective Writing

Conjunctions are important to effective writing for two key reasons: 1) They enhance the flow of writing by linking ideas, and 2) they show the relationships between pieces of information. When an author uses a conjunction in a sentence, they connect the ideas they are communicating to the reader, which makes the text flow more effectively with increased continuity. If writers did not use conjunctions, they would instead produce shorter, choppier sentences that lack the sentence fluency of works that use conjunctions effectively. In addition, the specific conjunction a writer selects is important because each conjunction sends a different message about the relationship between the pieces of information in the sentence. For example, the conjunction "and" shows that information being communicated is similar and has a lot in common, while the conjunction "but" signals a contrast between two pieces of information.

To further explore the impact of conjunctions on effective writing, let's look at the purposeful ways that published authors incorporate this tool in their works. In the book *Hair Love* (Cherry & Harrison, 2019), author Matthew

Cherry has the book's narrator Zuri use the conjunction "and" in the first line of the book: "My name is Zuri, and I have hair that has a mind of its own" (n.p.). In this sentence, the conjunction "and" links the statements and shows that they are both part of Zuri's identity. By sharing these pieces of information in her introductory remarks and connecting them with the conjunction "and," Zuri shows that these are ideas that are related in her mind. If a different conjunction was used in this sentence, the text wouldn't keep its original meaning and wouldn't make as much sense. For example, if the sentence used the conjunction "or" instead and read "My name is Zuri, or I have hair that has a mind of its own," it would communicate that only one of these statements is true, which would be both confusing to readers and not representative of what Zuri is trying to express. The conjunction "and" combines the information in this sentence in ways that are clear and are aligned with the text's message. In addition, if the sentence did not use any conjunctions, the text would not read as smoothly as it currently does. Without a conjunction, it would read "My name is Zuri. I have hair that has a mind of its own." While this sentence still conveys the same information, it is much choppier and less cohesive than the original text. The conjunction "and" helps the flow of the sentence while also showing readers the relationship between its key ideas.

Another effective example of a published author using a conjunction to connect ideas and show the relationship between pieces of information is found in the book *Carmela Full of Wishes* (de la Peña & Robinson, 2018). In this book, which describes the experiences of a girl named Carmela on her birthday, author Matt de la Peña uses the coordinating conjunction "but" in the passage, "Carmela knew exactly what manure was, but she didn't want to think about that. Not today." In this excerpt, the conjunction "but" plays an important role in the effectiveness of the passage. One reason for its significance is the way this conjunction combines the components of the sentence in which it's used. Without the conjunction "but," the sentence would read "Carmela knew exactly what manure was. She didn't want to think about that." These two short, choppy sentences don't have the same flow that de la Peña's original text does. Another benefit of this conjunction's use is that it shows that the two statements in the sentence in which it's used differ from each other. By placing the conjunction "but" between "Carmela knew exactly what manure was" and "she didn't want to think about that," the author shows that these two pieces of information are different. If Matt de la Peña instead wrote "Carmela knew exactly what manure was, so she didn't want to think about that," the sentence would suggest a similarity between the two statements. The conjunction "but" clearly shows their relationship.

As these examples from *Hair Love* (Cherry & Harrison, 2019) and *Carmela Full of Wishes* (de la Peña & Robinson, 2018) illustrate, conjunctions are important tools for effective writing. By using conjunctions in their works, authors can maximize the flow of their writing by connecting related statements and avoiding the use of short, choppy sentences. In addition, effectively used conjunctions show the relationship between the pieces of information the author combines. While these words may be small in size, they can make a big impact on the quality of a piece of writing!

We'll now take a look inside Kasey's classroom and see how she works with her students on the writing concept of conjunctions.

Classroom Snapshot

Kasey began the lesson by saying, "Today we are going to learn about conjunctions. That is another big word. Can you say 'Conjunctions?'" The students repeated the word. Kasey replied, "Way to go! Conjunctions are words that connect sentences together. For example, rather than saying 'I like apples. I like oranges.' I can use a conjunction and say, 'I like apples and oranges.'" Kasey directed students to look at the board and introduced Figure 7.1 by saying, "There are many different types of conjunctions but these are the ones that we are going to focus on." Kasey read each type of conjunction, the descriptions of usage, and the example sentences. Kasey emphasized that conjunctions connect ideas and help us avoid having short choppy sentences in our writing.

Kasey showed students the cover of the book *Carmela Full of Wishes* (de la Peña & Robinson, 2018) and said, "Today we are going to listen to a story about a girl. It is her birthday and she is finally old enough to go out exploring with her brother. She finds a dandelion and is thinking about all of the wishes that she could make. As you listen to the story, see if you can identify conjunctions. Remember, the conjunctions that we are focusing on are "and," "or," "so," and "but." Kasey began reading the story and stopped after the first few pages. Kasey reread the sentence, "Carmela knew exactly what manure was, but she didn't want to think about that" (n.p.) and highlighted the conjunction "but." Kasey continued reading the story and stopped after Carmela picked the dandelion outside the laundromat. She highlighted the use of "but" again and then continued on to finish reading the rest of the story. After reading, Kasey used Figure 7.2 to reflect on the conjunctions in the story. Kasey asked students, "Who can raise their hand and share a conjunction that they identified in the story?" A student raised his hand and said, "so." Kasey replied, "Excellent! Let's take a look back in the story and find where 'so' is used." Kasey recorded the word "so" on the graphic organizer and then returned to the story to find the example. Kasey read, ". . . imagining her dad getting his papers fixed so he could finally be home" (n.p.). Kasey continued, "The word 'so' is used in this sentence to show that until her dad got his papers fixed, he couldn't be home. One thing has to happen in order for the other thing to happen." Kasey revisited examples of the other conjunctions in the story and explained the reason for using each.

Since this is a little bit more of a complex concept for students, Kasey decided to work on creating example sentences as a class. Kasey said, "Now that we have learned about conjunctions and how to use them, we are going to work together to write sentences using the different conjunctions. Let's start with 'but.' Who can give me a sentence using the conjunction 'but?'"

Terri raised her hand and said, "I wanted to go outside, but my mom said no." Kasey replied, "Yes! Great thinking, Terri!" Kasey wrote the example on the board and then asked, "Who can give me another example?" Harper raised her hand and said, "It is hot, so we are going to go to the beach." Kasey responded, "Nice job, Harper." She recorded her example on the board and then continued to work with students to create examples using the other conjunctions. Kasey closed the lesson by saying, "Today we learned about conjunctions. We learned about a few types of conjunctions, what they mean, and how to use them. We listened to a story to see how the author used conjunctions to tell a story. Last, we worked together to create sentences using the different conjunctions. As you continue to develop your writing skills, I encourage you to try using conjunctions in your writing. Way to go, friends! Great thinking, kiss your brains!"

Recommendations for Teaching Students About Conjunctions

In this section, we share an instructional process that we recommend early elementary school teachers use when helping their students learn about conjunctions. The instructional activities that make up this process are designed to help students think about conjunctions as tools for effective writing. Throughout the process, students learn about what conjunctions are, think about why they're important to effective writing, practice using them, and reflect on their impact. The steps of this process are as follows:

1. Share with students key information about the features of conjunctions.

2. Show students published examples of conjunctions.
3. Talk with students about the benefits of the conjunctions used in the published texts.
4. Work with students as they incorporate conjunctions in their own writing.
5. Help students reflect on the importance of conjunctions to effective writing.

Let's now take a look at how these instructional steps can look in action.

Step One: Share With Students Key Information About the Features of Conjunctions

We recommend beginning this instructional sequence by introducing students to key information about what conjunctions are and the kinds of information they provide. By sharing these ideas with students, we begin to build their foundational knowledge of conjunctions and establish the groundwork for them to be successful throughout this process. To share these ideas with students, we recommend first introducing them to the key conjunctions described in this chapter: "and," "or," "so," and "but." One way to do this is to write the heading "Conjunctions" on an anchor chart and then write these four conjunctions below it. After you share these examples with students, we suggest introducing students to the essential uses of conjunctions with an explanation such as "Conjunctions are tools that writers can use to connect pieces of information. They're like bridges between ideas. When we're writing and we want to combine information, we can use conjunctions to do this."

After you share these examples and these introductory statements about the uses of conjunctions, we suggest using the information in Figure 7.1 to provide additional explanation of the features of each of these conjunctions. Using the ideas in the chart depicted in Figure 7.1, you can talk with students about each of the conjunctions "and," "or," "so," and "but, discussing how each one is used and sharing an example of it in a sentence. As you talk with students about each conjunction, we recommend returning to the previous anchor chart on which you wrote the conjunctions and writing a corresponding example of its usage next to the conjunction. When you write these sentences, you could use the examples depicted in Figure 7.1 (such as "We scored a lot of points, but our team still lost the game." for "but") or you can create your own examples that you think will align with students' interests and understandings. After you create this chart, we encourage you to display it on the wall of the classroom and to keep it there while your students work on conjunctions: it will provide a visual reminder that students can return to as they continue to engage with this concept.

Step Two: Show Students Published Examples of Conjunctions

This step of the instructional process helps students look at authentic uses of conjunctions in published texts. This practice provides students with real-world examples of how conjunctions are used and further helps them see these concepts as tools that can be used to enhance pieces of writing. To do this, we recommend reading to students from books that use one or more of the conjunctions you've introduced to your students and pointing out each conjunction as you read it. (While reading, we also suggest using a document camera to project the pages so that students can see the book's text as well.) For instance, if you read to students from the book *Eyes That Speak to the Stars* (Ho & Ho, 2022), you could highlight the conjunction "and" in the sentence "Your eyes rise to the skies and speak to the stars" (n.p.). By doing so, you would show students an authentic use of this conjunction, which would communicate to students that these grammatical tools are used by published authors in the works they create. Afterward, you could show students a different conjunction in a published text, such as the following sentence from *Opal Lee and What It Means to Be Free* (Duncan & Bobo, 2022), which uses the conjunction "but": "He danced a jig with cowboys playing fiddles, but they did not stop his flow" (n.p.). This sentence, which describes a young boy running through a picnic to get his grandmother, provides students with another example of a purposefully used conjunction in a published text. It further familiarizes them with the concept of conjunctions and shows them real-world instances of their usage. In addition, the published examples students see here prepare them for the next step of the instructional process, in which they'll consider the benefits of these conjunctions to the published texts in which they're used.

Step Three: Talk With Students About the Benefits of the Conjunctions Used in the Published Texts

This component of the instructional process helps students think carefully about the conjunctions in the published examples they saw in the previous step by discussing how each conjunction enhanced the sentence in which the author used it. To begin this conversation, we suggest talking with students about how this activity extends from the previous one; for example, you might say "We just looked at some examples of conjunctions in published writing. Now, we're going to think about why the authors of those books used the conjunctions they did. This will help us understand the benefits of those conjunctions." After you introduce the activity, we recommend returning to each published example you looked at in the previous step and working with students to identify the conjunction (or conjunctions) in it. Once you've done, we suggest asking for students' thoughts on why that conjunction was helpful to the sentence in which it appeared and why the author may have chosen to use it.

Sentence Containing a Conjunction	Conjunction Used in the Sentence	Benefits of Using This Conjunction

Figure 7.2 Conjunction Benefits Graphic Organizer

As you conduct these conversations with students, we encourage you to complete the graphic organizer depicted in Figure 7.2 and available in reproducible form in Appendix B; it asks you to write the sentence, identify a conjunction used in it, and reflect on the benefits of using that conjunction. (If a sentence has more than one conjunction, you can complete the conjunction identification and benefits more than once for that sentence.)

While the specific discussions that you and your students have for each conjunction will vary, two key ideas that can be useful to highlight in these discussions are the way that the conjunction connects information and the way that it shows the relationship between the pieces of information that it connects. For example, if you and your students are discussing the sentence "Your eyes rise to the skies and speak to the stars" (Ho & Ho, 2022, n.p.) from *Eyes That Speak to the Stars,* you can work with students to help them identify that this sentence links information and prevents the author from needing to write two short choppy sentences, such as "Your eyes rise to the skies. They speak to the stars." In addition, you can talk with and encourage them as they think about the way the conjunction "and" shows that the information in the sentences is similar and part of a series of connected ideas. If another conjunction, such as "but" or "or" was used, the sentence would indicate a different relationship between the information in it. By conducting these kinds of discussions with our students, we can further help them think of conjunctions as tools that authors purposefully use in their works.

Step Four: Work With Students as They Incorporate Conjunctions in Their Own Writing

At this point in the instructional process, students can take the knowledge they've developed about the features and benefits of conjunctions and apply those ideas to pieces of writing they create. To prepare and motivate students to do this, you might give them some introductory explanations that help them transition from the previous activity to the current one, such as "When we last talked about conjunctions, we thought about the conjunctions that published authors use and the reasons they use them. Today, we're going to take the next step: we're going to work on using conjunctions ourselves. I'll come around and help you as you use conjunctions in your work. I'm very excited to see what conjunctions you use!" After these introductory explanations, students can create sentences that contain one of the conjunctions you've discussed with them throughout the instructional sequence. When students create these sentences, they can work in a range of ways associated with their individual literacy levels and comfort levels with writing. For instance, they can write a sentence with a conjunction, dictate a sentence to the teacher, or draw a picture of one or more actions and verbally explain what is taking place in the sentence (while using a conjunction in the explanation). This variety of forms of communication provides students with flexibility in how they express their knowledge of conjunctions.

While students create these examples, we recommend holding individual writing conferences with them. During these conferences, you can provide students with needed writing support aligned with the method they're using to create their conjunction examples. In addition, we suggest talking with students about two key pieces of information: the conjunction they used and why they chose to use that conjunction. By communicating with students about these topics, you'll be able to assess their understanding of the concept of conjunctions. For example, if you talk with a student who uses the conjunction "so," you can evaluate their knowledge of the concept by first seeing if they identify the conjunction correctly. Next, when you ask the student why they chose to use that conjunction, you can listen to their explanation of why that conjunction aligns with the information in the sentence. If the information the student shares is accurate, then you know they have a strong understanding of the concept. If anything needs further clarification and explanation, you can use the conference to provide students with any other information that would help develop their understanding.

Step Five: Help Students Reflect on the Importance of Conjunctions to Effective Writing

After students have created sentences with conjunctions and conferred with you about them, we recommend concluding this instructional process by asking them to reflect on why conjunctions are important tools to effective writing. To guide students through the reflection process, we like to ask them two related questions: "Why are conjunctions important to effective writing?" and "When you use a conjunction, why is it important to think about the conjunction you use?" By helping students reflect on these questions, we take our instruction beyond traditional grammar teaching practices that focus on memorization: we help our students think in deeper ways about why conjunctions are important and the care that writers should take when selecting specific conjunctions. We believe that creating spaces and opportunities for students to think about the significance of the grammar tools they are studying can develop their knowledge of the concept and deepen their awareness of it. Helping students begin to think reflectively about these kinds of ideas in the early elementary grades will establish a foundation on which they can continue to build throughout their lives. For example, a student might reply to the question "Why are conjunctions important to effective writing?" by commenting on the ways conjunctions help sentences sound better and connect what authors want us to know. They might then reflect on the question "When you use a conjunction, why is it important to think about the conjunction you use?" by sharing their thoughts on the different ways that specific conjunctions are used. All of these thoughtful responses will build students' awareness of this concept and of grammatical tools in general.

Final Thoughts on Conjunctions

Here we share closing insights about conjunctions, such as information about the features of this concept, thoughts on its significance to strong writing, and insights to keep in mind when teaching early elementary students about it:

◆ Conjunctions are words that combine ideas or link statements in a piece of writing.
◆ The conjunctions we address in this chapter are the coordinating conjunctions "and," "or," "so," and "but."
◆ While all these conjunctions are used to connect ideas, they all have different meanings and therefore are used in different ways. Figure 7.1 in this chapter contains details about the meanings and usages of the described conjunctions.
◆ Conjunctions are important to effective writing for two key reasons:
  – They enhance the flow of writing by linking ideas.
  – They show the relationships between pieces of information.
◆ When teaching early elementary students about question words, we recommend following this instructional process:
  – Share with students key information about the features of conjunctions.

– Show students published examples of conjunctions.
– Talk with students about the benefits of the conjunctions used in the published texts.
– Work with students as they incorporate conjunctions in their own writing.
– Help students reflect on the importance of conjunctions to effective writing.

Figure 7.3 depicts this instructional process in an easy-to-follow flowchart.

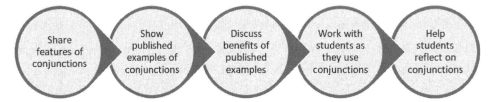

Figure 7.3 Conjunction Instructional Flowchart

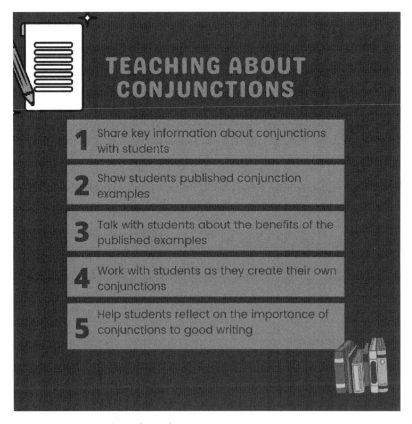

Figure 7.4 Conjunction Instruction Infographic

This infographic provides a visual representation of a mentor-text-based instructional process to use when teaching students about conjunctions.

This infographic displays conjunction mentor texts discussed in this chapter.

Mentor Texts for

Conjunctions

"My name is Zuri, and I have hair that has a mind of its own."
From Hair Love by Matthew Cherry and Vashti Harrison

"Carmela knew exactly what manure was, but she didn't want to think about that."
From Carmela Full of Wishes by Matt de la Peña and Christian Robinson

"Your eyes rise to the skies and speak to the stars."
From Eyes That Speak to the Stars by Joanna Ho and Dung Ho

Figure 7.5 Conjunction Mentor Text Infographic

8

More Than One

How Writers Indicate Plurals

What Are Plurals?

In this chapter, we'll examine the idea of plurals: forms of words that writers use to indicate that there is more than one of something. This concept connects to the topic of nouns discussed in Chapter 1—words that relate to people, places, things, or ideas. When we use a plural form in our writing, we're communicating to the reader that there is more than one of the person, place, thing, or idea we're describing. For example, we would say "dog" to show there is one, but we'd use "dogs" to indicate a plural. While the plural forms of many words are used by adding an "-s" to the end, there are a variety of ways that plurals are created. These different plural constructions depend on the features of the specific word being pluralized and are described in this section.

Plurals Formed by Adding "-s"

This is the most straightforward and intuitive way to create plurals in English. As previously stated, the plural forms of many words are formed by quickly and easily adding an "-s" to the end of the word, such as "bears," "lions," "pencils," and "desks."

Plurals Formed by Adding "-es"

In some situations, creating the plural form of a word involves adding "-es" to its end. While there are some exceptions, in general we add "-es" to the end

DOI: 10.4324/9781003302209-9

in words that end in the following ways: "s," "ss," "ch," "x," "and "sh." For instance, when changed to their plural forms, "bus" would become "buses," "inch" would become "inches," "box" would become "boxes," and "dish" would become "dishes."

Plurals Formed by Adding "-ies"
When a word ends with a consonant followed by the letter "y," such as "fly" or "puppy," we create the plural for that word by dropping the "y" and adding "-ies" to the end of the word. For example, "fly" would turn into "flies" and "puppy" would become "puppies." If a word ends in a "y," but the "y" follows a vowel (such as "key"), we just add an "s" to the word to create the plural (like with the word "keys").

Plurals Formed by Changing "f" to "ves"
Many words that end with the letter "f" or "fe" also change when they are turned into plurals; in this situation, we drop the letter "f" and conclude the word with the letters "ves." This plural form can be found with the word "leaf," which changes to "leaves" when it becomes a plural, and "knife," which becomes "knives" in its plural form.

Words That Don't Change in Their Plural Forms
Some words look the same in their plural forms, such as "deer," "fish," and "moose." Since they are identical whether they're singular or plural, the context in which they're used shows readers if the word refers to a singular or plural noun. For example, an author might say that "I saw a deer" when talking about one deer and could say "I saw five deer" when using the noun as a plural.

Irregular Plural Forms
Words that take irregular plural forms follow no real pattern when changing from a singular to a plural. Some commonly used words that take irregular plural forms are "mouse," which changes to "mice" in its plural form, "child," which changes to "children," and "goose," which changes to "geese."

Figure 8.1 lists the various plural types and provides examples of each type.

These examples illustrate that there are many ways that nouns take plural forms in English! As we'll discuss in more detail in the instructional suggestions later in this chapter, we encourage you to familiarize your students with the concept of plurals and some of the ways they look, but not overwhelm them with specific rules. What's most important is that your early elementary

Plural Type	Examples
Plural formed by adding "-s"	Singular: bear; plural: bears Singular: lion; plural: lions
Plural formed by adding "-es"	Singular: bus; plural: buses Singular: inch; plural: inches
Plural formed by adding "-ies"	Singular: fly; plural: flies Singular: puppy; plural: puppies
Plural formed by changing "f" to "ves"	Singular: leaf; plural: leaves Singular: knife; plural: knives
Words that don't change in their plural forms	Singular: deer; plural: deer Singular: moose; plural: moose
Irregular plural forms	Singular: child; plural: children Singular: goose; plural: geese

Figure 8.1 Plural Types and Examples

students are aware of the idea of plurals and their significance to effective writing, which we address in the next section.

Why Plurals Are Important to Effective Writing

Plurals are important tools for strong and clear writing because they allow writers to clearly express when there is more than one of something and to accurately describe situations in which this is the case. For example, if a writer wanted to show that a person has multiple dogs and is walking all of them, they might write "She is walking her dogs." However, without the plural form of dog, it would be much harder for the author to communicate this information. The author may write something like "She is walking a dog of hers, another dog of hers, and another dog of hers." The plural word "dogs" allows for this information to be expressed much more clearly and concisely. In addition, the concept of plurals helps authors differentiate between situations in which there is only one of something and when there is more than one. By using a singular form instead of a plural one, authors can express to the readers that they are referring to one thing. For example, if an author wanted to refer to a single building, they would use the singular form (such as "We looked at the building"). By contrast, if an author wanted to refer to multiple buildings, they would use the plural form to express this (as in "We looked at the buildings").

In the book *The Year We Learned to Fly* (Woodson & López, 2022), author Jacqueline Woodson effectively uses plurals to clearly communicate to readers when she is referring to more than one entity. For instance, in the sentence "Lift your arms, close your eyes, take a deep breath, and believe in a thing" (Woodson & López, 2022, n.p.), the plural forms communicate to readers when the author is referring to more than one thing and when she is referring to a singular entity. By adding the letter "s" to the conclusion of the words "arms" and "eyes," Woodson clearly communicates to readers that she is referring to multiple arms and eyes in this sentence. If she didn't use the letter "s" to clearly indicate these plurals, Woodson wouldn't express the sentence's information in the way she intended. In addition, the use of these plurals helps us not only to understand that Woodson is referring to multiple arms and eyes, but also to one breath and one thing later in the sentence. By using the letter "s" to indicate plurals in this sentence, Jacqueline Woodson helps us understand the information and lets us know when something is plural and when it is singular.

Another example of effective plural use is found in the text *Tomatoes for Neela* (Lakshmi & Martinez-Neal, 2021). The following sentence is noteworthy not only because it clearly and effectively uses plurals to indicate when there is more than one of something discussed, but also because it provides an excellent example of plural formations that go beyond only adding "s" to the end of a word: "Juicy ripe peaches, plump blueberries, golden corn topped with stringy silk so shiny, it looked like the hair on Neela's doll" (Lakshmi & Martinez-Neal, 2021, n.p). In this sentence, which describes fruit and vegetables available at a market, author Padma Lakshmi adds a "-es" to the end of "peach" to form the plural word "peaches." In addition, when creating the plural form of "blueberry," she drops the "y" at the end of this word and adds "-ies" to make "blueberries." This sentence provides a strong mentor text example of these various ways to construct plurals, making connections to how these word formations can look in authentic settings. In addition, these plural forms are important to the reader's understanding of the information in the sentence. If the author did not use plurals when discussing peaches and blueberries, the sentence would suggest there is only one peach and one blueberry at the market. The plurals used here help us comprehend the sentence accurately and enhance the piece's clarity.

These examples from *The Year We Learned to Fly* (Woodson & López, 2022) and *Tomatoes for Neela* (Lakshmi & Martinez-Neal, 2021) demonstrate the importance of effectively used plurals to strong writing. By clearly using plurals in their works, authors Jacqueline Woodson and Padma Lakshmi construct clear and easy-to-understand texts. Through the use of this concept, the authors convey to their readers when they are discussing more than one of something. Without the use of plurals, these pieces would be less effective and would be difficult to understand. Let's now follow up our discussion of the importance of plurals to strong writing with a look at how Kasey helps her students understand this writing tool.

📷 Classroom Snapshot

Kasey began the lesson by asking students, "Who remembers what a noun is? Raise your hand if you can tell us what a noun is." Students quickly raised their hands and Emma shared, "A noun is a person, place, or thing." Kasey replied, "That's right, Emma! Let's take a look at some pictures." Kasey created slides with pictures to introduce the concept to students. The first slide was a picture of one thing and the following slide was a picture of the same thing but more than one. For example, Kasey showed students the first slide and asked, "What do you see?" Students replied, "A dog!" Kasey went to the next slide and asked, "What do you see?" Students replied, "Puppies!" and "Dogs!" Kasey showed the next slide with one pencil. The following slide was a picture of colored pencils. The other slides consisted of pictures of a bus, buses, a leaf, leaves, a lion, and lions. Kasey shared, "Notice, all of these pictures are nouns. I showed you pictures of just one thing and then a picture with more than one of the same thing. When we have more than one of something, the word becomes plural. When you shared, 'pencils, buses, leaves, and lions' these are all examples of plurals." Kasey used Figure 8.1 to introduce the concept further. She started by saying, "We make words plural by changing the ending of a word, but it depends on what letters the word ends with. This can be a little bit tricky so we are going to talk about it, but I don't expect you to be able to remember all of this. As you get older, in first and second grade, you will learn more about this as your reading and writing continue to develop." Kasey read through the plural types and examples for each one.

Kasey introduced the book *The Year We Learned to Fly* (Woodson & López, 2022) and said, "This story is about a girl and her brother. Their grandmother encourages them to use their imagination. Let's see where their imagination takes them. As you listen to the story, see if you can identify plurals." Kasey began reading the story and stopped after the first few pages. She highlighted a few of the plurals and then continued on to read the rest of the story. After reading the story, Kasey directed students to Figures 8.2 and 8.3 to reflect on the plurals from the story. Kasey asked, "Who can share a plural that they identified in the story?" Molly raised her hand and said, "Arms and eyes!" Kasey recorded arms and eyes on the graphic organizer and replied, "Great listening, Molly! Arms and eyes are formed from the words 'arm' and 'eye.' We add an -s to the end of the words." Kasey went back to the story to find the example and discussed how the sentence would be different without the plurals. Another student raised their hand and said, "kids." Kasey recorded the example and discussed adding "-s" to the end of the word. Kasey recorded the word "lives" on the board and said, "Let's look at this word 'lives.' Lives is plural and refers to more than one life, the brother and sister's lives. The word 'life' has an 'f' which is changed to "ves. Again, it can be a little tricky to remember all of these 'rules' for how to create plurals but you will learn more about them later."

Kasey used Figure 8.1 to go back and review the different types of plurals. She explained to students, "Now that we learned about plurals and why plurals are used in writing, I want you to practice what you learned by writing some sentences." Kasey wanted to break down the concept and keep it rather simple for students to understand the basic concept: plurals represent more than one of something. Kasey gave the students a paper with two lines on it. To start she directed students by saying, "Point to the first line, the line at the top. I want you to write a sentence using a singular noun, one thing." Students began writing their sentences and Kasey walked around the room to support students. As they finished their sentences, Kasey asked for students to share. One student raised his hand and shared, "I can ride my bike." Another student shared, "I can tie my shoe." Kasey gave the next direction by saying, "Now, I want you to keep that same idea but make it plural, more than one." As Kasey walked around to observe students writing their sentences, she realized that at this point developmentally, it is complex for students to fully understand changing word endings to create plurals. She didn't want to focus on the spelling of their plurals, rather that they used the plural correctly in the sentence to identify the concept of more than one. When students were finished writing their sentences, they shared. Harper shared, "I saw leaves falling from the tree." Another student shared, "My friends have bikes." Kasey replied, "Nice work, friends!" She ended the lesson by saying, "Today we learned about plurals. We learned what plurals are and how they are created. We listened to a story to see how an author used plurals in their writing and highlighted some of the examples from the story. Then, you used what you learned to write sentences, including a singular noun, one thing, and a plural. I challenge you to continue to see where you can identify plurals and practice using them in your own writing. Great work today! Thank you for your help!"

Name _Molly_____

I kot wif a eot.
    cook   with   pot

I hap x a gots.

I haf sum eats.
  have some   pots

Name _Kaelih_____

                        went
Me and my dad what
                    went
xon a hick.
     hike

Me and my mom
    went   vacation
What xon rckashih and
We what xon three hicks,
     went   hikes

Recommendations for Teaching Students About Plurals

Now that we've examined the ways that plurals are formed, why they are important to effective writing, and how Kasey engages her students in this concept, we'll share some instructional recommendations to use when teaching early elementary students about the writing concept of plurals. These recommendations combine to create an instructional process designed to help students think about the features of plurals, the impact they have on strong writing, and how they can incorporate this concept in their own works. This instructional process consists of five steps:

1. Talk with students about the ways that plurals are formed.
2. Show students published examples of plural words and work with them to identify the way the plural is created.
3. Discuss with students why the plural words in the published examples are important to the reader's understanding of the text.
4. Support students as they create works containing plurals.
5. Help students reflect on the importance of plurals to effective writing.

As students engage with this process, they'll become increasingly familiar with the features and importance of plurals, which they can use to enhance their writing in your class and well into their future work. Let's check out each of these instructional steps in detail.

Step One: Talk With Students About the Ways That Plurals Are Formed

To get students started thinking about the concept of plurals, we suggest having a conversation with them about the ways that we create plurals when we write. When beginning this conversation, we recommend connecting to students' background knowledge and previous experiences with the concept to help contextualize the idea of plurals. One way to do so is with the aid of familiar visuals that relate to how students may have used plurals in their everyday lives. For example, you might show them a picture of one dog and another picture of three dogs and then ask for students to tell you what's in each picture. After students share that the first picture has one dog and the second picture shows three dogs, you can connect this explanation to the concept of plurals with a statement such as, "When we say that this picture contains three dogs, we're using a plural. We use plurals when we want to show that there is more than one of something. Today we're going to start to talk about plurals and what they are."

Following this introductory connection, we recommend creating an anchor chart that identifies the concept of plurals and explains that they show when there is more than one of something. Afterward, we suggest sharing with students that there are a variety of ways that writers show something is a plural, using the information in the opening section of this chapter and in Figure 8.1 to indicate these different forms. As with the other grammatical concepts we've discussed in this book, we encourage you to present these ideas to students, but not to overwhelm students with the information or require them to immediately memorize these ways to create plurals. We recommend then creating an anchor chart like Figure 8.1 that identifies plural formations and examples so that students can refer back to this information throughout the instructional process. You might even note that there is a range of methods for creating plurals and that students will have plenty of time to continue to think about this concept with a statement such as, "The most common way to show that something is a plural is to add an '-s' to the end of a word, but there are some other ways also. We'll look at more examples of all these ways to make plural forms and even practice some of our own as we keep working on this. Great job today getting started with plurals!"

Step Two: Show Students Published Examples of Plural Words and Work With Them to Identify the Way the Plural Is Created

Now that students have been introduced to the concept of plurals and the ways they can be constructed, we recommend following up on this initial discussion by making connections to the ways they are used in published texts. To do this, we recommend sharing with students some published examples of plural words and then working with the students to identify the way that the plural of that word is created. This instructional practice has a number of benefits; one is that it shows students authentic examples of this grammatical concept, which indicates that the concept is used in real-world situations to make writing as effective as possible. In addition, it provides students with an opportunity to apply the ideas of plural form constructions that you introduced them to in the last activity. By looking at these published examples of plurals and discussing the ways the plural form was constructed, students can develop their understanding of this concept while engaging with authentic applications of it.

For example, in the book *Change Sings* (Gorman & Long, 2021), author Amanda Gorman uses plural words that are constructed in a range of ways. In the excerpt "I scream with the skies of red and blue streamers. I dream with the cries of tried and true dreamers" (Gorman & Long, 2021, n.p.), Gorman uses four plural words: "skies," "streamers," "cries," and "dreamers." Two of these plurals are formed by only adding "-s" to the end of a word— "streamers" and "dreamers"—and two are formed by dropping the "y" at the end of a word and replacing it with "ies"—"skies" and "cries." If you share

Plural Word from Published Text	How the Plural Form of the Word Is Created

Figure 8.2 Graphic Organizer: Plural Words and Constructions

this passage with your students, you could read it out loud and collaborate with them to identify the plural words in the sentence. To do so, you could ask for student volunteers to identify any plurals they see and help them notice any that they don't initially spot. After that, we encourage you to write down each plural word and to talk with students about the way the plural is constructed in that word. To guide this discussion, you can use the graphic organizer depicted in Figure 8.2 and available in reproducible form in Appendix B. This graphic organizer asks you to identify the plural word you notice and to explain how the plural is created.

For instance, when you identify the word "skies" as a plural, you would then write "Drop 'y' and add 'ies'" for the explanation of how the plural form of the word is created. Then, after identifying "streamers" as a plural, you could write "Add 's' to the end of the word" for how the plural is made. Completing this chart with your students will help them notice plural words and think about the specific way each one is formed.

Step Three: Discuss With Students Why the Plural Words in the Published Examples Are Important to the Reader's Understanding of the Text

In this third step of the instructional process, you'll work with students to talk about the importance of the plural words in published examples to the texts in which they appear. When discussing the significance of these words, we recommend emphasizing the ways that an author's use of plurals is important to the reader's ability to understand the text. You can transition to this activity by sharing with students how this discussion extends from and builds upon the work they did in the previous activity, with an explanation such as "When we last talked about plural words, we looked at examples of plurals from published writing and talked about how those plurals were created. Now, we're going to go even further with plurals: we're going to think about the published examples we discussed last time and talk about why those plurals are important tools for helping us understand what the author is saying. We'll be thinking about why plurals are important to creating writing."

To engage students in this work, we suggest first returning to a published passage containing plurals that you discussed in the previous instruction and re-read it for students. After you read the passage aloud, we recommend reviewing which words in the passage are plurals and identifying them. Next, we encourage you to write on a piece of chart paper "How do these plurals help us understand the information in the passage?" and then explain to students that they'll be exploring this question with you. To facilitate this discussion, you can rewrite the original published passage with singular words in place of plural forms and show both the original and the revised version to students. For example, the text "I scream with the skies of red and blue streamers. I dream with the cries of tried and true dreamers" (Gorman & Long, 2021, n.p.) would be rewritten as "I scream with the sky of red and blue streamer. I dream with the cry of tried and true dreamer." After you show these passages to students, we recommend asking them "Why do you think the plurals are important to the original passage?" As students respond, you can help them reflect on how the plurals clearly show readers when the author is referring to more than one thing. For example, the word "dreamers" is important to the text because it helps readers understand that author Amanda Gorman is talking about multiple dreamers instead of just one. To help students compare the original and revised version of the text, you can use the graphic organizer depicted in Figure 8.3 and available in Appendix B. This resource contains space to write the original version of a passage, a revised version without plurals, and students' reflections on the importance of the plural words.

Original Published Text	Text Without Plurals	Why the Plural Forms Are Important to the Original Text

Figure 8.3 Plural Reflection Graphic Organizer

Step Four: Support Students as They Create Works Containing Plurals

In this component of the instructional process, students transition from thinking about the features and importance of published examples of plurals to applying this concept to their own works. To do so, students can work at their individual literacy levels to create a phrase or sentence that includes one or more plurals. For instance, students can write a plural phrase (such as "two cats"), write a sentence with at least one plural in it, dictate to the teacher a plural phrase or a sentence containing plurals, or draw a picture that shows a plural (such as an image of two cats playing) and verbally explain what is taking place in it. Before students begin creating these examples, we suggest revisiting the initial anchor charts and information you shared in the first step of this process to remind them of the ways that plural forms can be created; reviewing these ideas can help students apply the various plural constructions to their writing.

While students work to create their plural examples, we encourage you to confer with them to monitor their progress and provide them with support. During these conferences, we suggest first asking students to identify the plural or plurals they are using in their work. This will help you ensure that students understand what plurals are and how to use them while also creating an opportunity for you to clarify any misunderstandings students may have about what a plural is or how it is formed. For example, if a student identifies a word as a plural that is not actually a plural form, you can help them create the plural form of that word. In addition, if a student constructs a plural in a different way from how the plural form of that word is constructed (such as forming the plural of "puppy" as "puppys" instead of "puppies"), you can revisit the anchor charts and other information you previously shared with them to help them create the plural of that word. These conferences provide excellent opportunities for individualized instruction for our students.

Step Five: Help Students Reflect on the Importance of Plurals to Effective Writing

To conclude this instructional process, we recommend asking students to think about the importance of plurals to effective writing. By engaging in this reflection, students will deepen their understanding of both the concept of plurals in general and the purposeful reasons that writers use them in their works. We feel that this reflective work benefits students as both readers and writers: thinking carefully about the importance of plurals can help students understand why the authors of the books they read use them and can help students purposefully incorporate this concept into their writing. To facilitate students' reflections on the importance of the concept of plurals, we recommend asking them to consider these two questions: "Why are plurals important to good writing?" and "How would writing be different if we didn't use plurals?" These questions can help students think about the importance of plurals and their key role in clear and effective writing.

As students reflect on these questions, we encourage you to help them think about the ways that plurals help authors clearly express when there is more than one of something in their works. In addition, students can think about how writing would be unclear without plurals and would likely be confusing for the reader. For example, the sentence "I took a walk and saw two dog." could confuse readers because they would wonder why the plural form of dog wasn't used. These reflection questions can help students further understand the impact of plurals on clear and effective writing. By developing this deepened awareness, students can be even more likely to feel confident with this writing tool.

Final Thoughts on Plurals

In this concluding section, we share some essential ideas to keep in mind about the writing concept of plurals and the instructional approach we recommend using with students when helping them understand, use, and reflect on this grammatical tool:

◆ Plurals are forms of words that indicate there is more than one of something.
◆ There are a variety of ways that plurals are created depending on the features of the specific word being pluralized. The possible forms and an example of each are listed here:
  – Plural formed by adding "-s" (Example: bears)
  – Plural formed by adding "-es" (Example: buses)
  – Plural formed by adding "-ies" (Example: puppies)
  – Plural formed by changing "f" to "ves" (Example: leaves)
  – Words that don't change in their plural forms (Example: deer)
  – Irregular plural forms (Example: children)

◆ Plurals are important tools for strong and clear writing because they allow writers to clearly express when there is more than one of something.
◆ When teaching early elementary school students about plurals, we recommend using this instructional process:

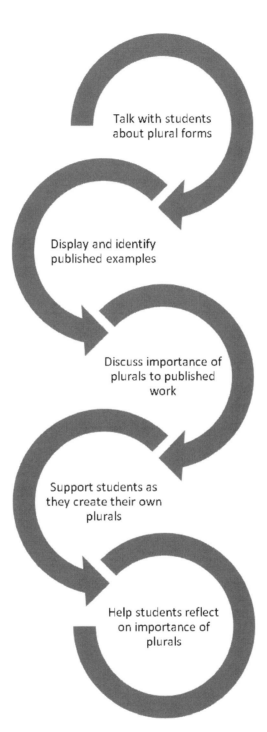

Figure 8.4 Plural Instructional Flowchart

- Talk with students about the ways that plurals are formed.
- Show students published examples of plural words and work with them to identify the way the plural is created.
- Discuss with students why the plural words in the published examples are important to the reader's understanding of the text.
- Support students as they create works containing plurals.
- Help students reflect on the importance of plurals to effective writing.

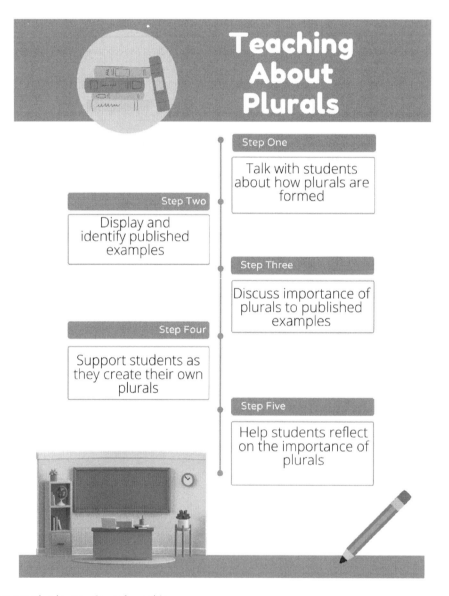

Figure 8.5 Plural Instruction Infographic

Figure 8.4 depicts this process in an easy-to-follow flowchart.

This infographic provides an engaging visual representation of a mentor-text-based instructional process to use when teaching students about plurals.

This infographic displays key plural mentor texts discussed in this chapter.

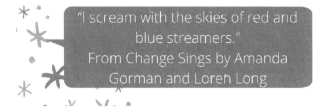

Figure 8.6 Plural Mentor Text Infographic

9

Tools for Clear Communication

The Importance of Commas

What Are Commas?

In this chapter, we'll explore an important writing tool that writers use to provide clarity and structure to their works: the concept of commas (,). Commas are punctuation marks that are placed within a sentence or a statement to separate pieces of information (rather than at the end of a sentence like the end punctuation marks of periods, question marks, and exclamation points described in Chapter 4 of this book.) While there are a variety of specific situations in which commas are used in writing, in this chapter we focus on three fundamental and important examples of comma use that align with the needs of early elementary school writers and many early elementary grade standards: commas that separate items in a series, commas used in dates, commas used in the greetings and closings of letters. Let's now take a look at each of these types of comma use.

Commas That Are Used to Separate Items in a Series

When listing a series of three or more items (such as animals, people, foods, or anything else they'd like to list), writers use commas to separate those things. For example, in the sentence "I played on the swing set, seesaw, and slide." the commas are used to separate the three types of playground equipment on which the speaker played. It's important to note that commas that differentiate between items in a series are only present if there are three or more items. If a writer lists two items instead, they are joined by the conjunction "and"

DOI: 10.4324/9781003302209-10

and the comma is not used. For example, in the sentence "I played on the swing set and seesaw." there isn't a need to use a comma to separate the items.

Commas That Are Used in Dates

Another important way that commas are used in effective communication is when writing dates, such as "Sunday, May 1, 2022." In this situation, commas are used between the day of the week and the month, as well as between the date and the year. The commas that are used in dates separate these key pieces of information. This comma usage is useful for early elementary students as they are beginning to record this information on assignments and daily activities.

Commas That Are Used in the Greetings and Closings of Letters

The third example of purposeful comma use that we'll examine in this chapter is commas that are used in the greetings (also called salutations) and the closings (also called valedictions or signoffs) of letters. Commas are used in letters' salutations after the recipient's name, such as "Dear Joe," and between the closing word or words and the writer's name, like "Sincerely, Michael." These examples of comma use can help students clearly structure important aspects of letter writing.

Figure 9.1 identifies these three types of comma use, describes the usage, and provides examples of each.

Now, let's think further about the importance of purposeful and strategic comma use to effective writing.

Type of Comma Usage	Description of Usage	Example
Commas that are used to separate items in a series	Commas are used to separate items in a series of three or more.	"They like to play football, baseball, and basketball."
Commas that are used in dates	Commas are used in dates between the day of the week and the month. They are also used between the date and the year.	Saturday, September 3rd, 2022
Commas that are used in the greetings and closing of letters	Commas are used in the greeting of a letter after the recipient's name. They are used in the closing between the closing word or words and the letter writer's name.	Dear Mom, Love, Frank

Figure 9.1 Key Types and Examples of Comma Use

Why Commas Are Important to Effective Writing

Commas are an important tool for effective writing because they are used to organize and separate ideas and information. While all three types of comma usage described in this chapter differ in some of their specific implementations, the common thread in all of them is that they distinguish between key pieces of information in the written works in which they're used. For example, when using commas in a series, a writer will use these commas to separate the items being mentioned. One example of this comma usage in a published text is in the book *Watercress* (Wang & Chin, 2021). In this picture book, there are multiple occasions when author Andrea Wang uses commas to separate three items in a series and clearly indicate that the identified things are separate from each other. One instance is in the following excerpt, which describes the paint on an older car: ". . . the red paint faded by years of glinting Ohio sun, pelting rain, and biting snow" (Wang & Chin, 2021, n.p.). In this passage, commas separate the three elements of nature that have faded the paint, which clearly conveys to the reader that these are all separate. If Andrea Wang had instead written "the red paint faded by years of glinting Ohio sun pelting rain and biting snow," the lack of commas would make it much more difficult to understand; it would be harder for readers to distinguish between the three things Wang mentions. By using commas to separate the items in this series, Andrea Wang helps readers comprehend the information in the passage much more easily.

The importance of commas to clear and effective writing is also present in the following passage from the book *The Story of Jackie Robinson* (Thorpe, 2021), which uses a comma to separate information in a date: "Jack Roosevelt Robinson was born on January 31, 1919" (n.p.). In this excerpt, author Andrea Thorpe placed a comma between "31" and "1919" to clearly distinguish between these components for the reader. The use of this comma lets us know that 31 is the date of the month and 1919 is the year when the event took place. If the author instead wrote "January 31 1919," the piece could be confusing for readers since the comma would not be there to clearly separate the information. This comma ensures clarity in the piece and helps readers understand the date in the way the author intended it to be understood.

Another example of comma usage facilitating clarity in a piece of writing is present in the book *Dear Reader* by Tiffany Rose (2022). This picture book, which is structured like a letter, contains the statement "Dear Reader, do you see that little girl down there?" (Rose, 2022, n.p.). In this passage, the comma after "Reader" separates the greeting (or salutation) of the letter from the rest of the text and provides a clear structure that helps the reader understand the information. If the piece instead read "Dear Reader do you see that little girl down there?," it would be more difficult for readers to make sense of the piece. Without this comma, it's more difficult to tell where the greeting ends and the rest of the text begins. This comma enhances the reader's experience by making sure that the piece is clear and easy to understand.

These examples from *Watercress* (Wang & Chin, 2021), *The Story of Jackie Robinson* (Thorpe, 2021), and *Dear Reader* (Rose, 2022) illustrate the importance of commas to clear and effective writing. By using commas in strategic and purposeful ways, these authors provide readers with works that are easy to understand. While these published examples use commas in different ways—one passage uses them to separate items in a series, one uses a comma to clearly express the information in dates, and another uses a comma to distinguish between the greeting of a letter and the text in it—all of them use this concept as a tool for clear and effective writing that helps writers separate information and provide their readers with pieces that they can easily comprehend and enjoy. Without commas, all of these published works would be less clear and understandable than they are. Let's now look at how Kasey works with her students on the writing concept of commas.

📷 Classroom Snapshot

Kasey began the lesson by saying, "Emma, when we read *Bilal Cooks Daal* (Saeed & Syed, 2019) and learned about complete sentences, you asked me, 'What is that thing that looks like a 9?' and I explained that it was a comma and we would talk about them later." Kasey said, "Friends, today we are going to learn about commas. Commas are a type of punctuation. We also learned about that big word 'punctuation,' but commas are not at the end of sentences." Kasey directed students to the board and used Figure 9.1 to introduce the concept of commas. She said, "You have probably seen commas many times but just didn't know what they were called or why they were there." She introduced the type of usage to separate items in a series and referred back to *Bilal Cooks Daal* (Saeed & Syed, 2019) and said, "This is the type of comma that Emma asked me about when the author listed the different spices that Bilal was using to cook daal. Using a comma helps the writer avoid having to use the word 'and' repetitively." Kasey introduced the usage in dates and directed students to look at the calendar where the date was displayed. She pointed out the commas used to separate the day, month, and year. After she explained the types of comma and usage of each, and gave examples, it was time to look at how an author uses commas in their writing.

Kasey introduced the book *Dear Reader* by Tiffany Rose (2022) and said, "Now we are going to listen to a story to see how an author uses commas in her writing. This story is about a girl who loves books but wants more books with diverse stories and people, people from all walks of life. As you listen to the story, see if you can identify any commas." Kasey began reading and stopped after the first page to highlight the comma used at the beginning of the story and explained how it is an example of an opening of a letter. Kasey continued reading and stopped when the girl was explaining the different kinds of books she likes, "Big books, small books, thin books, and tall books. Books about fish, alligators, science, and shells. Books of thrones, queens, friendship, and dreams." (Rose, 2022, n.p.) She said, "This is similar to our example with Bilal and the spices. She is listing a series of three or more types of books; therefore, she uses a comma to separate the ideas and make it easier for us, the readers, to understand the story." Kasey continued reading the rest of the story. After reading the story, Kasey used Figure 9.2 to reflect on the examples of commas from the story. Kasey located examples from the story and discussed the different components of the graphic organizer with students.

Now that students had a better understanding of the use of commas, it was time for students to apply their learning into their writing skills. Kasey wanted to focus on commas that are used to separate items in a series. She reminded students, "When we have a series of things, we use a comma between each thing to separate the ideas and avoid using the word 'and' over and over again." She pulled up the Student Assessment Graphic Organizer and explained, "I want you to write a sentence in this box (Kasey drew an arrow pointing to the box "Use the example in a sentence") and draw a picture to match your writing in the box (Kasey drew a star next to the box with "Draw a picture of what's happening in the sentence"). Like last time, I will help you with the other boxes." Students began writing and Kasey went around the room to support students. One student wrote, "I like oranges, grapes, and bananas." She discussed with students the concept of a comma, the example of its use in a series of things, and that without the use of a comma it would be more difficult to understand the sentence. As students finished, Kasey asked for them to read their sentences and share with the class. Kasey closed the lesson by saying, "Today we learned about commas. We learned about the three types of commas, how they are used, and looked at examples of each. Then, we listened to a story to see how an author uses commas in their writing. We reflected on the examples of commas from the story and discussed how they were used and why they are important. Last, you took what you learned and wrote a sentence using commas. As you continue to explore books and develop in your writing, I challenge you to identify commas within books or in examples around you. Also, see if you can use commas in your own writing. Way to go friends, nice work!"

Emma

Concept:	Example:
Commas	in a series

Use the example in a sentence:

I like teddy bears
Slime and squishies
Slime / squishies

Draw a picture of what's happening in the sentence:

Slim

Why the example of the concept is important to the sentence:

Hah Peh

Concept:

Commas

Example:

in a series

Use the example in a sentence:

In the wintn timeI
                                    coat   some   gloves
wane a ckowt, sum gluvs,
and a hat.

Draw a picture of what's happening in the sentence:

Why the example of the concept is important to the sentence:

Recommendations for Teaching Students About Commas

Now that we've considered key information about commas, explored their importance to effective writing, and learned from Kasey's classroom practices, let's examine a step-by-step instructional process designed to familiarize students with the uses of commas, help them understand their importance to effective writing, and empower them to effectively use them in their own works. This process contains five steps that build on each other to help students learn about and utilize this grammar tool:

1. Introduce students to commas and key concepts related to their usage.
2. Share with students published examples of comma usage and discuss the comma concepts they represent.
3. Talk with students about the impact of commas on the effectiveness of the published examples.
4. Support students as they use the comma concepts you shared with them.
5. Help students reflect on why commas are important tools for effective writing.

By engaging in this process, students will deepen their understanding of commas and become increasingly familiar with this important concept. Let's now look at these instructional steps in detail.

Step One: Introduce Students to Commas and Key Concepts Related to Their Usage

In the first step of this instructional process, we suggest helping students build fundamental understandings of what commas are and some ways they're used. To begin students' work with this concept, we recommend drawing a comma on a piece of anchor chart paper and sharing an introductory statement such as: "The punctuation mark here is a comma. It's the next writing tool that we're going to talk about together. You may have seen commas around school, like in the books in our classroom and on signs around the building. Writers use commas to separate information when they write." Underneath the comma drawn on the anchor chart, we suggest then writing "Commas: Tools that writers use to separate information." After you've shared these opening statements with students, you can identify the specific comma uses that you and the students will be thinking about by making a statement such as, "There are a lot of ways that authors use commas to separate information. In our work together, we're going to think about three key ways that writers use commas, which we'll start to look at now."

Next, we suggest displaying another anchor chart that lists the three forms of comma uses that are discussed in the beginning of this chapter and in Figure 9.1. As you introduce students to each of these ways that commas are used, we recommend explaining that all three of these examples are ways that commas separate pieces of information, with a statement such as "In the first of these examples, commas are used to separate things in a list. In the second one, they're used to separate parts of a date. In the third one, the commas are used to set apart sections of a letter. Even though they're a little different from each other, all of these are times when commas separate information." As we've discussed with other concepts in this book, we like to focus this opening explanation as a way to introduce students to information, but not feel overwhelmed by it. To help with this, you can emphasize to students that they'll be continuing to learn more about commas as they continue to work and that this is just the starting point. To support students as they keep working through this instructional process, we suggest hanging these comma-focused anchor charts on the classroom wall and telling students that the information is hanging there so that they can continue to look back on it as they keep learning about commas.

Step Two: Share With Students Published Examples of Comma Usage and Discuss the Comma Concepts They Represent

Once you've introduced students to information about the concept of commas and key examples of their usage, we recommend incorporating published examples of this concept into the learning process. By showing students published texts that use commas in these ways, we communicate that these comma concepts are used by real-world writers in authentic situations. In addition, providing students with published examples of these comma concepts helps them practice with the information while seeing the ways that published authors use them, which can be more engaging and meaningful than out-of-context examples, such as those found on worksheets. To engage students in this work, we recommend showing them three published examples of comma usage and, after displaying and reading aloud each example, asking them which comma rule it represents. This activity calls for students to apply the comma concepts they're studying to the published examples with which they're engaging.

There are a range of published texts that represent these comma concepts; during this activity, you can use the examples described earlier in this chapter to demonstrate what these concepts look like, or you can select other instances of their use to discuss with students. Commas that separate items in a series can be found in texts of all genres, while the other two forms are more aligned with particular genres: commas that are used in dates are often found in informational texts and those used in the greetings and closings of letters are present in that form of writing. One strong example of commas used to set apart items in a series is in the following excerpt from the article "Cotton-Top Pop" from *Ranger Rick* magazine. In this article, which describes the primate species the cotton-top tamarin, author Hannah Schardt uses commas to separate information in a list of items in the animal's diet: "The rest of their diet may not sound so scrumptious to you: insects, spiders, sap, and the occasional lizard" (Schardt, 2017, p. 28). At another point in this same *Ranger Rick* magazine issue, commas are used in the greetings of letters: all of the letters that readers write to the magazine are in a section that begins "Dear Ranger Rick," (p. 4). In the greeting "Dear Ranger Rick," the comma after "Rick" separates this part of the letter from the rest of the text. Now, let's turn to another informational magazine and another example of comma use: the article "Stump Your Parents: Presidents Edition" in the February 2021 issue of *National Geographic Kids* uses commas to distinguish between components of a date in the trivia question, "Which two presidents both died on July 4, 1826—the 50th anniversary of the Declaration of Independence?" (p. 29). The comma between "4" and "1826" separates these parts of the date.

When using these examples—or others like them—in the classroom, we recommend showing students each excerpt individually and asking them what comma concept it represents. We suggest encouraging students to look back at the anchor charts as they consider the published examples you show them. They can then use the anchor chart examples and explanations, as well as their own insights, to determine which comma concept aligns with each published example. As students share their identifications, it's important to ask them why they think the published example being discussed corresponds with the comma concept they've identified. For example, if students look at the sentence "The rest of their diet may not sound so scrumptious to you: insects, spiders, sap, and the occasional lizard" (Schardt, 2017, p. 28) and identify it as an example of commas that separate items in a series, you can encourage them to identify the items in the series that are separated and the commas that separate those items. This helps students think about the comma-related concepts they are studying and prepares them for the next step of this instructional process, in which students think about the impact of the commas in these published examples.

Step Three: Talk With Students About the Impact of Commas on the Effectiveness of the Published Examples

Now that students have seen and identified examples of the comma concepts addressed in this chapter, we recommend further engaging them in this topic by helping them think about and reflect on the importance of the commas to the published examples they examined in the previous step. This activity is designed to help students think about commas as important tools to effective writing that authors use to maximize the effectiveness of their works. By engaging in this reflection and analysis, students can think in in-depth ways about how commas make writing stronger, clearer, and more effective. To begin this instructional step, we recommend displaying the published comma examples you showed students in the previous activity and explaining that the class will be looking at these examples again, but in a different way. You might share an explanation such as: "You all did such a great job looking at published examples of commas and thinking about the ways those commas were used. Now, we're going to take our work another step further: we'll look at the same published examples and talk about why it's important that the authors used the commas they did."

To guide students through this work, we suggest displaying each published example of comma use, rewriting it without commas, and asking students to respond to two questions related to it: "Why is using commas important to this example?" and "How is the example different when we take the commas away?" To facilitate this discussion, we recommend using the graphic organizer in Figure 9.2; this chart contains space for you to rewrite the original published text, a revised version of the text without commas, and students' responses to each of the reflection questions. (A reproducible version of this chart is also available in Appendix B.)

For example, if you used the sentence "Which two presidents both died on July 4, 1826—the 50th anniversary of the Declaration of Independence?" (p. 29) from the February 2021 issue of *National Geographic Kids* magazine for

Original Published Sentence	Published Sentence Without Commas	Reflection: Why Is Using Commas Important to This Example?	Reflection: How Is the Example Different When We Take the Commas Away?

Figure 9.2 Graphic Organizer for Published Comma Examples and Student Reflections

this activity, you would first write the original sentence and then rewrite it without the comma between "4" and "1826," forming "Which two presidents both died on July 4 1826—the 50th anniversary of the Declaration of Independence?" After you show both examples to students, you can lead a discussion with them in which they share why they think the commas are important to the sentence. Students might note that the comments are important to the sentence because they separate the day and the year and make it clear when one ends and the other starts. Finally, students can think about how the sentence is different without the commas. In their responses, they might explain that the sentence without commas is harder to understand and doesn't clearly separate the day and year. You can use this same pattern of comparison and reflection to help students think carefully about the role that commas play in effective writing and their importance to clear and well-structured works.

Step Four: Support Students as They Use the Comma Concepts You Shared With Them

At this stage, students apply the awareness and understanding about effective comma use that they've developed throughout the instructional process. We recommend helping students apply their knowledge of commas by setting up three stations for them, each of which is focused on students creating examples of the comma concepts they've explored in this instructional process. For example, one station would be dedicated to students creating work that uses commas to separate items in a series, another would focus on giving students practice using commas in dates, and a third station would provide students with a chance to use commas in greetings and closings of letters. As students work at each station, they can focus on using that station's focal concept in ways that align with their individual levels of familiarity and comfort with writing. For instance, students could dictate text to the teacher and state where commas should go, begin to write as much as they're comfortable and then dictate and explain the rest, or write the text and commas themselves.

As students work at these stations on creating examples of the focal comma concepts, we recommend conferring with them to gauge their understanding of the concept and provide them with any needed support. During these conferences, we suggest asking students to show you the commas they used and to explain to you why they used them in those locations. By looking at where students placed commas and listening to their explanations, you can learn a great deal about their understanding of comma usage and how well they're able to apply the concepts you've explored with them. For example, during these conferences, you can look at where students placed commas in their examples; if the commas they used don't align with the comma concepts you've discussed with them, you can support them and help them clarify any confusion. If the students are using the commas accurately, you can compliment their work and talk with them about why those commas are used effectively. With all students, these individualized writing conferences provide opportunities to monitor how students are doing with the concept and to support them in individualized ways.

Step Five: Help Students Reflect on Why Commas Are Important Tools for Effective Writing

We recommend concluding this instructional process by creating opportunities for students to reflect on the importance of commas to effective writing. This culminating activity is designed to help students think in even more depth about the significance of this writing tool and the role that it plays in clear and strong pieces of writing. It builds off the work students did in the third step of this instructional process, when they thought about the impact of commas on published examples, but takes this reflection to an even higher level by asking students to think about not only the specific examples they looked at that time, but the concept of commas in general. We suggest introducing this reflective work by recapping what students have done up to this point in the instructional process and then presenting the questions that students will consider as part of this activity, with an explanation such as, "You've done such a wonderful job thinking about commas! We've talked about three ways writers use commas, looked at those examples in published writing, thought about why the commas the published writers used were important, and practiced using them on our own! Now, we're going to talk about two questions that will help us think even more about the importance of commas."

After you share this introductory explanation, we encourage you to display the following reflection questions that the students will answer: "Why are commas important tools for effective writing?" and "How would writing be different if writers didn't use commas?" As students respond to the first question, you can help them think about how commas are important to effective writing because they organize and separate ideas and information. When they comment on the second question, we suggest helping them reflect on and discuss the ways that information in writing wouldn't be as clearly structured without commas. For example, they can think about how writing without commas would be harder to distinguish between items in a list, identify different components of dates, or find the greetings and closings of letters. By thinking in reflective ways about these key ideas related to comma use, we can help our students deepen their knowledge of this writing tool.

Final Thoughts on Commas

In this closing section, we share key ideas to keep in mind from this chapter on comma use, such as important features of this concept, insights on its impact on effective writing, and ideas to consider when teaching early elementary students about the attributes, uses, and importance of commas:

◆ Commas are punctuation marks that are placed within a sentence or a statement to separate pieces of information.
◆ While there are a variety of specific situations in which commas are used in writing, in this chapter we focus on three fundamental and important examples of comma use that align with the needs of early elementary school writers and many early elementary grade standards:
  – Commas that separate items in a series.
  – Commas used in dates.
  – Commas used in the greetings and closings of letters.

◆ Commas are an important tool for effective writing because they are used to organize and separate ideas and information.
◆ While all three types of comma usage described in this chapter differ in some of their specific implementations, the common thread in all

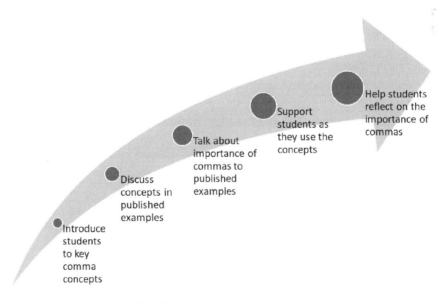

Figure 9.3 Comma Instructional Flowchart

Figure 9.4 Comma Instruction Infographic

Figure 9.5 Comma Mentor Text Infographic

of them is that they distinguish between key pieces of information in the written works in which they're used.

◆ When teaching early elementary students about commas, we recommend following this instructional process:

  – Introduce students to commas and key concepts related to their usage.

– Share with students published examples of comma usage and discuss the comma concepts they represent.
– Talk with students about the impact of commas on the effectiveness of the published examples.
– Support students as they use the comma concepts you shared with them.
– Help students reflect on why commas are important tools for effective writing.

Figure 9.3 depicts this instructional process in an easy-to-follow flowchart.

This infographic conveys a mentor-text-based instructional process to use when teaching students about commas.

This infographic depicts some comma mentor texts discussed in this chapter.

10 ⚒

We Are Writers

How and Why Writers Use Pronouns

What Are Pronouns?

In this chapter, we focus on another important tool for effective writing that can help the literacy development of early elementary school students: the concept of pronouns, which are words that take the place of a noun in a piece of writing. Remember in Chapter 1 when we discussed nouns: they are words that are used to refer to people, places, things, or ideas. Nouns can also be common (meaning that they are general people, places, things, or ideas, such as "city") or proper (which means they are specific examples of those nouns, such as "Miami"). Pronouns can stand in for any of these types of nouns, which makes them very frequently used words in writing.

While there are a variety of types of pronouns that can be used in writing, in this chapter we focus on the personal pronouns "I," "we," "you," "they," "she," "he," and "it." These pronouns are called subjective case personal pronouns, which means they are used to refer to people, places, things, and ideas that are the subjects of sentences or clauses. They are among the most widely used pronouns in the English language and provide an important foundational starting point for students as they learn about this writing tool. Figure 10.1 provides an example of how each of these personal pronouns can take the place of nouns in sentences: the chart depicted in this figure contains each pronoun, a sentence that does not use the pronoun, and a revised version of the sentence in which the pronoun takes the place of a noun.

DOI: 10.4324/9781003302209-11

Pronoun	Sentence That Does Not Use the Pronoun	Revised Sentence in Which the Pronoun Takes the Place of a Noun
I	"Sean likes running," Sean said.	"**I** like running," Sean said.
We	Janet and I are taking a walk.	**We** are taking a walk.
You	"Brody did well on the test," the teacher told Brody.	"**You** did well on the test," the teacher told Brody.
They	Sawyer and Greyson are outside.	**They** are outside.
She	Kasey is a teacher.	**She** is a teacher.
He	Jake ordered a milkshake.	**He** ordered a milkshake.
It	The milkshake is delicious.	**It** is delicious.

Figure 10.1 Key Pronoun Examples and Their Uses

As we share fundamental information about pronouns with our early elementary students, it's essential that we take an inclusive perspective on pronoun usage. Pronoun use is evolving in the interest of being inclusive of all gender identities; it's important we educators are aware of this and keep it in mind as we work with our students (Ruday, 2020a, 2020b).

The National Council of Teachers of English (NCTE)'s (2018) Statement on Gender and Language provides important information on the development of language and ways teachers can approach language instruction in inclusive ways, especially regarding pronoun use. This NCTE statement recommends using inclusive phrasing such as "Each cast member should know their lines by Friday" instead of binary-oriented phrasing such as "his or her lines."

When introducing students to the key features of pronouns, it's important to approach this concept with an inclusive perspective. This will help create a classroom environment that is respectful of individuals' identities and uses language as a tool of inclusivity rather than exclusivity. For instance, the NCTE statement advises that "When referring to any individual, respect that individual's chosen pronoun usage, or lack thereof." Approaching pronouns from a place of respect and inclusivity is important to building a strong and supportive classroom environment. For more information on NCTE's Statement on Gender and Language, please visit https://ncte.org/statement/genderfairuseoflang/.

Figure 10.2 A Note on Pronouns

Why Pronouns Are Important to Effective Writing

Pronouns are important tools for effective writing because they reduce repetition and maximize sentence fluency. For example, if a writer didn't use any pronouns, a description of the action of a basketball game might look like this: "Jeff made a basket, and then Jeff high-fived a teammate. Jeff was excited that the team was winning." In this example, the name "Jeff" is used three times in a short passage, creating a great deal of repetition in the piece and making it sound clunky and awkward for readers. A revised version of this passage that uses pronouns to make the piece less repetitive and more fluid reads as follows: "Jeff made a basket, and then he high-fived a teammate. He was excited that the team was winning." In this version, the use of the pronoun "he" eliminates the repetition of the name "Jeff," which makes the piece easier to read and helps the ideas flow together more effectively.

Published authors purposefully use pronouns as tools for these purposes, incorporating them in their works to eliminate repetition and create fluency in their writing. For example, in the book *Amy Wu and the Perfect Bao* (Zhang & Chua, 2019), author Kat Zhang strategically uses the pronoun "she" to make the following passage as effective as possible: "Amy can do a lot of things. She can brush her teeth. She can tie her shoe" (n.p.). If Zhang did not use any pronouns in this excerpt, the resulting text would be "Amy can do a lot of things. Amy can brush her teeth. Amy can tie her shoe" (n.p.). While this version contains the same basic information, it doesn't provide as smooth and clear an experience for readers. The repetition of the word "Amy" makes the passage feel more cumbersome and tedious to read. The use of pronouns solves this problem by varying the language used in the text and providing readers with a more pleasant experience.

Another example of a published author effectively using pronouns to maximize the effectiveness of a piece is the following passage from *Oona* (DiPucchio & Figueroa, 2021), which introduces the book's main character, a mermaid named Oona: "Oona was sweet . . . and a little bit salty, like the ocean where she lived. She was also brave and curious, like most treasure hunters" (n.p.). The uses of the pronoun "she" in this passage help the piece flow together well without unnecessary repetition. If the text instead read "Oona was sweet . . . and a little bit salty, like the ocean where Oona lived. Oona was also brave and curious, like most treasure hunters," readers would not have the same high-quality experience with the piece. Without pronouns, these sentences lack the variety that the original text does; the text not only repeats the name "Oona" a great deal, but also begins both its sentences in the same way. By using pronouns in this text, author Kelly DiPucchio provides readers with variety in the language used in the piece and in the way these opening sentences begin.

In both *Amy Wu and the Perfect Bao* (Zhang & Chua, 2019) and *Oona* (DiPucchio & Figueroa, 2021), the use of pronouns makes a significant impact on the text. It eliminates repetition and creates fluid, cohesive sentences that are smooth, clear, and varied. These examples help illustrate that pronouns are important tools for effective writing that can give readers the best experience possible with a text. Now, let's look at an example of Kasey working with her students to help them understand the writing concept of pronouns.

📷 Classroom Snapshot

Kasey began the lesson by saying, "Let's think about nouns again. Remember, a noun refers to a person, place, or thing. Common nouns refer to general people, places, and things like my teacher, the park, or the store. Proper nouns refer to a specific person, place, or thing, like Ms. Haddock, Mt. Trashmore, or Target. A pronoun can take the place of a noun. Today, we are going to learn about personal pronouns." Kasey directed the students to the board and used Figure 10.1 to introduce the concept. She read through each pronoun and discussed the sentences with and without pronouns. She emphasized the importance of personal pronouns by saying, "Personal pronouns are important to avoid repetition, using the same word over again. For example, rather than saying 'Ms. Haddock is my kindergarten teacher. Ms. Haddock teaches me new things. Ms. Haddock lets us play and have fun.' I can use personal pronouns and say, 'Ms. Haddock is my kindergarten teacher. She teaches me new things. She lets us play and have fun.' By doing so, I avoid saying 'Ms. Haddock' over and over again."

Kasey introduced the book *Oona* (DiPucchio & Figueroa, 2021) and said, "Now that we have learned a little bit about pronouns, let's take a look at how an author uses pronouns in their writing. This story is about a mermaid who loves to search for treasure. As you listen to the story, see if you can identify any pronouns. Remember, some of the pronouns we learned are I, we, you, they, he, she, it." Kasey began reading the story. She stopped after the first few pages introducing Oona and said, "Notice the author uses Oona's name and then uses the pronoun 'she' to avoid saying her name every time." Kasey continued to read and then stopped after the author introduced Otto and said, "Now the author uses the pronoun 'they' to avoid saying Oona and Otto every time." Kasey continued reading the rest of the story. After reading the story, Kasey used Figure 10.3 to reflect on the pronouns from the story. She began the discussion by asking, "Who can raise their hand and share a pronoun that you identified or remember from the story?" Weslei raised her hand and shared, "She!" Kasey replied, "Very good! Let's take a look back at the story and find where the author uses that pronoun." Kasey directed the students back to the story to discuss "she" and recorded their reflections on the graphic organizer. Kasey asked for another pronoun from the story and Emma raised her hand and shared, "They!" Kasey replied, "Yes, great thinking!" Again, she directed students back to the story to locate the examples and recorded them on the board. Kasey turned to the end of the story and said, "Let's look at this page again and see if you can identify the pronoun used." She read from the book, " 'We did it!' Oona cheered, placing the crown on her best friend." (DiPucchio & Figueroa, 2021, n.p.) and then asked, "Can you identify the pronoun in that sentence?" Kaelin raised her hand and said, "We." Kasey replied, "That's right! The author uses 'we' in this sentence when Oona is celebrating her and Otto finding the treasure. 'We' refers to Oona and Otto." Kasey recorded the example and its importance on the graphic organizer.

Kasey used Figure 10.1 to go back and review the different pronouns and how they are used. Kasey said, "Now that we know and understand what pronouns are and how they are used, I want you to apply what you have learned into your own writing." Kasey decided to keep things simple and focus on personal pronouns referring to people. She gave students lined writing paper and said, "I want you to write a sentence about someone you know. It could be about you and someone else or just them. Use their name and tell me something about them." Students began writing their sentences and Kasey walked around the room to support any students who needed help. Kasey then said, "Now I want you to think about that person and write another sentence about them using a pronoun. If you wrote a sentence about you and someone else, think about what pronoun you would use." When students finished writing, Kasey directed them to draw a picture to match their writing. Once students were finished, Kasey directed students to put their materials away to show they were ready to share their writing with the class. Kasey collected the papers and displayed students' papers one at a time under the document camera for the class to see. Each student read their sentences and shared. Weslei shared, "Terri and I like to play outside. We go to the park." Kaelin shared, "My mom and dad like to travel. They took a trip to Florida." Kasey praised students for their hard work and closed the lesson by saying, "Today we learned about pronouns. We learned about the different types of personal pronouns and how they are used. We listened to a story to see how an author uses pronouns in their writing. After reading, we went back to the story to identify examples of pronouns and why they are important. Then, you took what you learned and applied it to your own writing. As you continue to explore reading through a variety of books, see if you can identify examples of pronouns. I also challenge you to use pronouns in your writing. Excellent work today, friends! Thank you for your help!"

Recommendations for Teaching Students About Pronouns

In this section, we present an instructional process to use when teaching early elementary school students about the features, importance, and uses of pronouns. This instructional sequence is designed to help students grasp the concept of pronouns, consider their impact on published texts, use them in their own writing, and reflect on their significance as a writing tool. It consists of the following five steps:

1. Share with students key information about pronouns.
2. Show students published examples of pronoun usage.
3. Talk with students about the importance of pronouns to the published texts.
4. Confer with students as they use pronouns in their own works.
5. Work with students as they reflect on the importance of pronouns to effective writing.

Now, let's take a look at each of these instructional recommendations in depth.

Step One: Share With Students Key Information About Pronouns

We recommend beginning this instructional process by talking with students about some fundamental ideas regarding pronouns. The goal of this instructional step is not to bombard students with information or encourage them to memorize a number of pronoun-related details, but instead to activate any background knowledge they have about the topic and establish foundational information on which you'll build throughout the process. We suggest beginning this initial step by showing students that pronouns are concepts used in everyday communication; this can then help students feel more comfortable and familiar as they think about the information you'll share with them about the topic. For example, Sean might begin by saying to students: "My son Sawyer played baseball all day yesterday. He really loves baseball." After sharing this information and writing it on the whiteboard, Sean would call attention to the pronoun he used in the sentence: "In this statement, I used the pronoun 'he' in the second sentence when I referred to my son Sawyer. Pronouns are words that we use a lot when we speak and write. Today, we're going to start thinking about some examples of pronouns. You might notice some that you use when you talk and write also."

After providing students with initial information like this that frames the pronoun-related work they'll do and presents the concept in an accessible and relatable way, we suggest introducing students to the personal pronouns identified in the first section of this chapter and presented in Figure 10.1. To share this information with students, we recommend creating two anchor charts: one that lists each of these six personal pronouns and another that provides examples of how all six of these pronouns can look in sentences. To create the example sentence anchor chart, you can use sentences in Figure 10.1 or create your own examples. For example, the sentence in Figure 10.1 that uses the pronoun "we" is "We are taking a walk." By providing students with these anchor charts and displaying them in a prominent location during this instructional process, you'll create accessible resources for them to use throughout their work with pronouns.

Step Two: Show Students Published Examples of Pronoun Usage

Once you've introduced students to the pronouns that you'll be exploring in this instructional process, we recommend showing them some authentic examples of how they're used in published texts. To do this, we suggest reading aloud from a book that you feel your students will find engaging and accessible and identifying examples of the personal pronouns you discussed in the previous step. (If possible, we also recommend displaying the text on a document camera so that you can point to the pronouns while you read them.) For example, if you read to your students the book *Islandborn* (Díaz & Espinosa, 2018), you can highlight the following passage that uses the pronoun "she" multiple times: "Lola, you see, loved to draw, but she left the island when she was just a baby so she didn't remember any of it" (n.p.). As you share this example with students, we suggest calling attention to each pronoun in the text. After this, we recommend sharing with students another published example that uses different pronouns than the first one so that they can see other pronouns in published works. For instance, in the book *We Are in a Book!* (Willems, 2010), author Mo Willems uses the pronoun "we" at a number of points in the book, such as in the passage "We are in a book! We are being read!" (pp. 20–21). Sharing examples like these will increase students' familiarity with the concept and provide them with a number of published examples of the pronoun types they're exploring in this instructional process. In addition, this activity adds authenticity and validity to the work that students are doing with pronouns by showing students that these concepts are tools that published writers incorporate in their work. All of these learning benefits will serve students well in the next step of this instructional process, in which students will think about the benefits of pronouns to published texts.

Step Three: Talk With Students About the Importance of Pronouns to the Published Texts

After students have seen published examples of effective pronoun use, we recommend engaging them in conversations about the importance of these published pronouns to the texts in which they appear. To help students think about this topic, we suggest returning to the published examples you showed them in the previous step and talking with them about key pronouns used in each example, how that passage would look without those pronouns in it, and why they think those pronouns are important to the passage. By addressing these topics with students, you can help them think in reflective ways about the writing tool of pronouns and the ways they can make writing better. To engage students in these discussions, we recommend using the graphic organizer in Figure 10.3; it contains space to identify the original published sentence, list key pronouns used in it, rewrite the sentence without those pronouns, and record students' insights on why those pronouns are important to the text. (A reproducible version of this form is also available in Appendix B). This graphic organizer is designed to be used with one published sentence at a time; if you and your students analyze multiple sentences, you can use a different graphic organizer with each sentence.

For example, if you and your students use the sentence from *Islandborn* (Díaz & Espinosa, 2018) discussed in the previous instructional recommendation, you would first write the original text: "Lola, you see, loved to draw, but she left the island when she was just a baby so she didn't remember any of it" (n.p.). After this, you can identify the pronoun "she" as a frequently used personal pronoun in the sentence and then rewrite a new version that does not contain this pronoun, such as "Lola, you see, loved to draw, but Lola left the island when Lola was just a baby so Lola didn't remember any of it." After you read this revised version to students, you can talk with them about how all of the uses of "she" in the original piece are replaced with "Lola" in the new sentence and ask them why the uses of the pronoun she are important to the original sentence. As students respond, you can help them call attention

Original Published Sentence	Key Pronouns Used in the Sentence	Sentence Without Those Pronouns	Why Those Pronouns Are Important to the Passage

Figure 10.3 Graphic Organizer: Published Pronoun Analysis

to how repetitive the revised sentence without pronouns is and how the sentence containing pronouns is much easier to read. By thinking with you about these ideas, students can deepen their understanding of the importance of pronouns to the published texts you've shared with them.

Step Four: Confer With Students as They Use Pronouns in Their Own Works

At this point in the instructional process, we recommend turning even more ownership over to students by asking them to create their own works containing pronouns. This activity builds off of the work students have done throughout this process (such as learning about key pronoun types, examining published uses of them, and thinking about their importance to published writing), but adds an additional component: students' constructions of their own examples. To do this, we recommend asking students to create a short passage of one or two sentences that uses one of the personal pronouns addressed in this instructional process. Before students begin creating their works, we suggest introducing the activity by summarizing what they've done and showing them examples of what they might compose. For example, you might say something like, "You've done such a wonderful job with pronouns! I love how carefully you thought about why the pronouns are important to the published examples we saw! Now, you're going to get to practice making your own examples that contain the pronouns we've discussed. Here is an example with the pronoun 'we': 'My mom and I are watching a Halloween movie because we love Halloween.' See how in that example I used the pronoun 'we'? In your example, you'll use one or more pronouns. I'll check in with you and answer questions while you work to help you use the pronouns we discussed in your own pieces."

To account for students' varying literacy levels, we recommend creating a number of opportunities for students to create these pronoun-infused passages, such as writing a sentence containing a pronoun, dictating a sentence containing a pronoun to the teacher, drawing a picture that represents an image or action and verbally describing it using as a pronoun, or writing as much of a sentence containing a pronoun as possible and dictating the rest. While students work, we recommend checking in with them and holding individual conferences that are designed to monitor their progress and provide them with personalized support. During these conferences, we recommend asking students to do two things: 1) Identify the pronoun they used in the piece, and 2) explain why they chose to use that pronoun. By answering these questions, students will show you how accurately they understand pronouns and their thought process regarding how they select the best pronoun for each situation. If students' responses demonstrate any confusion or any ideas that can be further developed, you can talk with them about these ideas and help them deepen their awareness of what pronouns are and how writers select them.

Step Five: Work With Students as They Reflect on the Importance of Pronouns to Effective Writing

We recommend concluding this instructional process with a reflective activity in which students think about and share their ideas on the importance of pronouns to effective writing. To introduce this activity, we suggest explaining how it extends from the work that students have done up to this point with pronouns. For example, you might say to students, "We've done wonderful work together with pronouns and have done so many things with them! I love the way you created your own pronoun examples in our last activity. Today, we're going to a final activity with pronouns that will help you think about and understand them even more. We're going to think about why pronouns are so important to good writing."

To help students engage in this reflection, we recommend displaying two questions for them: "Why do you think pronouns are important to good writing?" and "How do you think writing would be different if authors didn't use pronouns?" After introducing these questions to students, you can then ask them to think about and respond to each one. When students reflect on the first question, we recommend helping them think about the ways pronouns make writing less repetitive and easier to read. In their responses to the second question, we suggest helping students identify and think about similar ideas, such as the ways writing would be much more repetitive without pronouns and how the redundancy and awkwardness of sentences that use the same nouns over and over again would not be as enjoyable for those who read it. By reflecting on these ideas associated with the importance of pronoun use, our students can continue to think about pronouns as key tools that authors use to maximize the effectiveness of their works. These insights will help them strategically and intentionally use this writing tool—both in your class and in their future writing.

Final Thoughts on Pronouns

This final section summarizes major points from this chapter, such as key features of pronouns, their impact on effective writing, and instructional practices for helping early elementary school students learn about this writing tool:

- ◆ Pronouns are words that take the place of a noun in a piece of writing.
- ◆ While there are a variety of types of pronouns that can be used in writing, in this chapter we focus on the personal pronouns "I," "we," "you," "they," "she," "he," and "it."
    - – We've selected these because they are among the most widely used pronouns in the English language and provide an important foundational starting point for students as they learn about this writing tool.
- ◆ Pronouns are important tools for effective writing because they reduce repetition and maximize sentence fluency.
- ◆ It is important to approach the concept of pronouns from a place of respect and inclusivity. Figure 10.2 in this chapter and the NCTE Statement on Gender and Language (2018) provide examples of phrasings and pronoun usage that align with an inclusive perspective on pronoun usage that avoids gender binaries and respects individuals' pronouns.
- ◆ When teaching early elementary students about the grammatical concept of pronouns, we recommend following this instructional process:
    - – Share with students key information about pronouns.
    - – Show students published examples of pronoun usage.
    - – Talk with students about the importance of pronouns to the published texts.

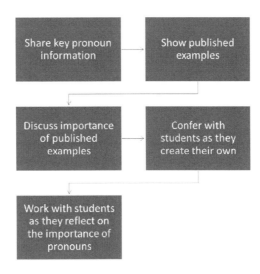

Figure 10.4 Pronoun Instructional Flowchart

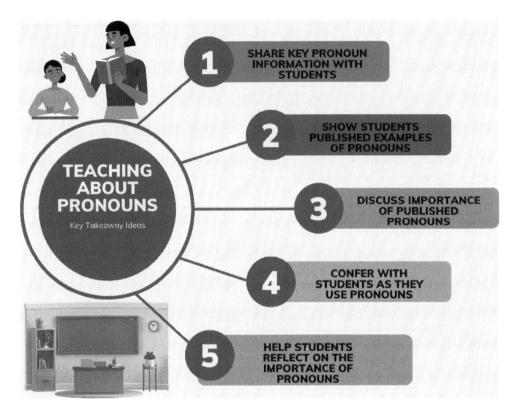

Figure 10.5 Pronoun Instruction Infographic

    – Confer with students as they use pronouns in their own works.
    – Work with students as they reflect on the importance of pronouns to effective writing.

Figure 10.4 depicts this process in a flowchart.

This infographic provides an engaging visual representation of a mentor-text-based instructional process to use when teaching students about pronouns.

This infographic depicts key pronoun mentor texts discussed in this chapter.

Figure 10.6 Pronoun Mentor Text Infographic

11 🔧

Assessing, Learning, and Growing

Assessing Students' Knowledge

What We Believe About Grammar Assessment

In this chapter, we focus on the best ways to assess students' knowledge of grammatical concepts. Our approach to grammar assessment is asset based (Gibson, 2020), which means that it focuses on students demonstrating their knowledge in ways that are authentic and meaningful, providing opportunities for students to show their awareness of what grammatical concepts are and why they're important. In contrast, a lot of traditional grammar assessment is deficit based (Lanehart, 2002) and out of context (Wotjer, 1998), meaning that it doesn't connect to real-world uses of concepts and focuses more on students' mistakes than the ways they show their knowledge in authentic and relevant ways. As we describe in this chapter, we support grammar assessment that provides students with engaging and meaningful opportunities to demonstrate their understanding of what grammatical concepts are, how they're used, and why they're important to effective writing. This assessment approach extends logically and naturally from the instructional practices described in this book: just as those teaching recommendations value authentic uses of grammatical concepts and corresponding reflections, the assessment practices discussed here represent those same values and ideas. Now, let's take a look at the details of the assessment approach we recommend using.

DOI: 10.4324/9781003302209-12

What Effective Grammar Assessment Can Look Like

To assess early elementary school students' understanding of what grammatical concepts are, how they're used, and why they're important to effective writing, we recommend using a graphic organizer that asks students to demonstrate their knowledge of these ideas. A template for this graphic organizer is depicted in Figure 11.1; it asks for students to identify an example of the concept on which students are being assessed, use it in a sentence, draw a picture of what's taking place in that sentence, and explain why the concept is important to the sentence. The activities on this graphic organizer provide students with opportunities to demonstrate their understanding of grammatical concepts, show their awareness of how the concepts look in sentences, visualize how the concept is used in the sentence by drawing a picture, and comment on the importance of this concept to the sentence in which it's used. In addition, the opportunities to create examples and draw corresponding pictures provide students with opportunities to incorporate their own interests through relevant examples that are embedded in the assessment. (A reproducible version of this graphic organizer is also depicted in Appendix B.)

After you engage students in the instructional processes described in this book for each grammatical concept, you can ask them to complete this graphic organizer for the concept so that you can assess their knowledge of it and provide them with any needed support and instruction. For example, when you and your students have completed the instructional process focused on verbs, students can fill out this graphic organizer to demonstrate their understanding of the features, uses, and importance of verbs. You can identify verbs as the focal concept on the graphic organizer and then ask students to create an example of a verb, use that example in a sentence, draw what's taking place in that sentence, and comment on why the concept is important to the sentence. For instance, a student could identify the verb "sprint" as an example, create a sentence such as "She will sprint to the finish line," draw a picture of a runner moving quickly toward a finish line of a race, and reflect on how that verb shows the reader the action taking place in the sentence. Similarly, if students are working with the concept of capitalization, they can create a capitalized word, use it in a sentence, draw a corresponding picture, and reflect on the significance of that word to the effectiveness of the sentence. In addition, you can differentiate these assessments for students by creating opportunities for them to verbally dictate their examples, sentences, and reflections; this will provide students with a variety of ways to express their understanding of the features and importance of grammatical concepts.

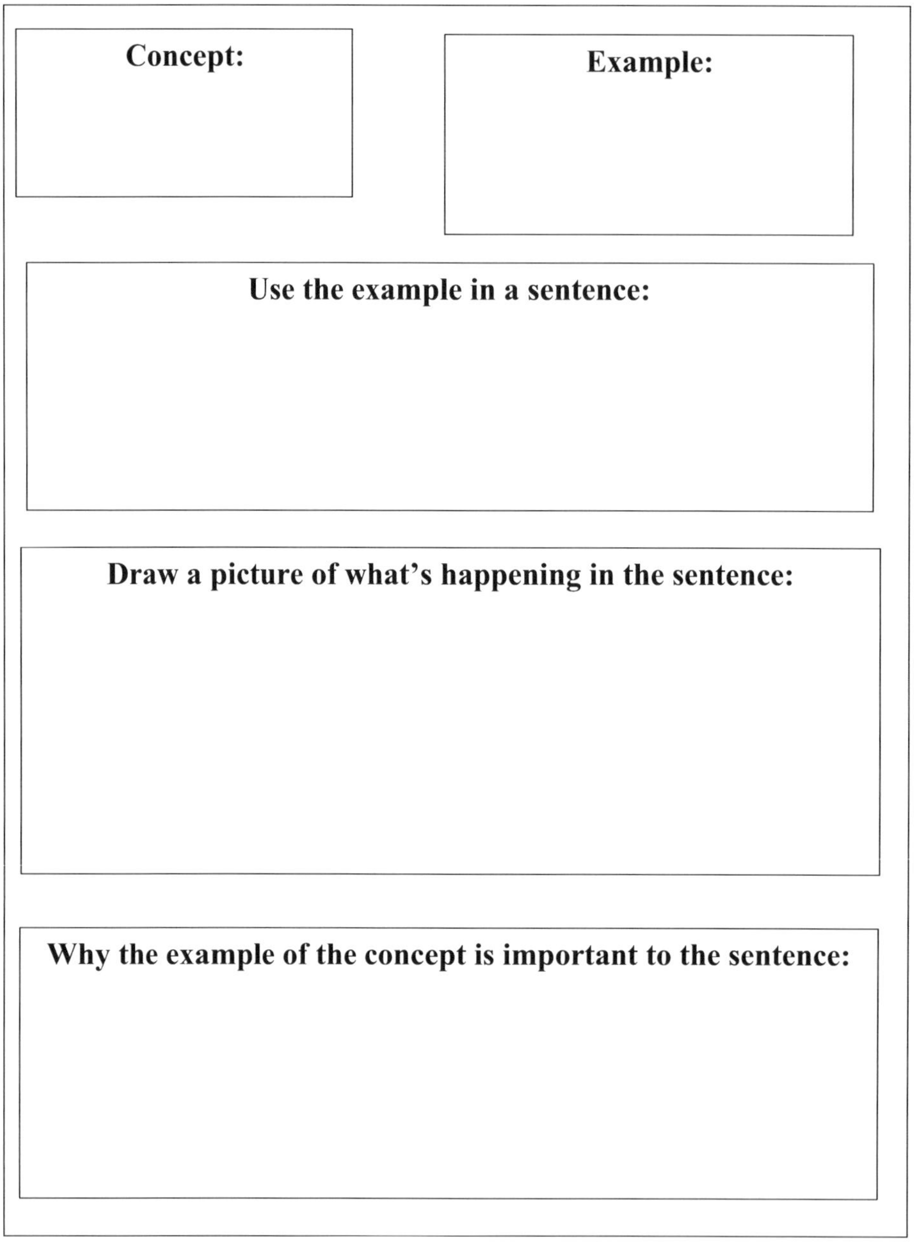

Concept:		Example:

Use the example in a sentence:

Draw a picture of what's happening in the sentence:

Why the example of the concept is important to the sentence:

Figure 11.1 Student Assessment Graphic Organizer Template

This is in a separate document called Student Assessment Graphic Organizer Template. An image of the graphic organizer template follows as well.

This graphic organizer provides a resource for students to use as they demonstrate their knowledge of a grammatical concept. This organizer contains five blocks for students to complete: one in which they identify the concept, another for them to write an example of the concept, a block for them to use the example in a sentence, one in which they draw a picture of what is happening in the sentence, and finally a space for students to indicate why the example of the concept is important to the sentence the student created. This image is also available on the book's website as downloadable Support Material.

Evaluating Students' Work on These Assessments

An important aspect of incorporating these assessments of students' understanding of grammatical concepts is thinking about the most useful and effective assessment criteria to use when evaluating their work. We encourage you to evaluate students' work on these assessments by considering the following ideas: the accuracy of the examples that students create, the ways that the sentences demonstrate effective use of the example, and the detail and thoughtfulness of the students' explanations of the importance of the concepts to the sentences in which they are used. These assessment criteria are aligned with the instructional approach described in this book—they privilege students' applications of the grammatical concepts they've studied and their reflections on the importance of those concepts. Figure 11.2 depicts a sample rubric that you can use when evaluating your students' work on these assessments. It contains opportunities to score and comment on students' examples, their

Component and Explanation	Score (Out of four points for each category)	Comments
Accuracy of example • Is the example of the grammatical concept accurate? • Does it show an understanding of what the concept is?	/4	
Use in a sentence • Is the concept used accurately and effectively in a sentence? • Does the use of the concept in a sentence show an understanding of the concept?	/4	
Explanation of the importance of the concept to the sentence • Is the explanation of the importance of the concept detailed and informative? • Does it demonstrate a strong understanding of the concept?	/4	

Total score: /12
Concluding comments:

Figure 11.2 Sample Assessment Evaluation Rubric

uses of those examples in sentences, and their reflections about the importance of those examples. (A reproducible version of this rubric is available in Appendix B.)

In this rubric, students' work on each category is scored between one and four, with a maximum of twelve total points. There is also a space at the bottom to write concluding comments about students' performance. Based on students' performance on this assessment, you can identify any concepts or information within those concepts that you might need to reteach. For instance, if a student has used a pronoun effectively, but needs support thinking about why it is important to the sentence, you can revisit the significance of the concept in your instruction. If a student is struggling with creating an example of a concept or having difficulty with accurately identifying it, you can revisit the topic with that student and help them understand its features so that they develop this understanding.

Final Thoughts on Effective Grammar Assessment

Assessing students' knowledge on grammar is an important aspect of the process of teaching and learning grammar. The assessment graphic organizer and rubric described in this chapter will help you evaluate your students' understandings of grammatical concepts in ways that facilitate their success with this subject, help them see them elements of grammar as tools that can develop the effectiveness of writing, and give you useful information that can inform your future instruction. The assessment approach we present here is based on the principles of authenticity, support, use, and reflection described in the instructional activities in this book. Just as the instructional methods we discuss frame grammar instruction in an authentic way by focusing on real-world uses of those concepts and their role in effective writing, these assessments ask students to think about these grammatical tools in similar ways. These application- and reflection-based assessment processes are designed to facilitate student success in positive and productive ways. The examples that students create align with real-world uses of grammatical concepts and the reflections they compose are designed to help students think about these concepts in meaningful and lasting ways.

Conclusion

Final Thoughts and Tips for Classroom Practice

Throughout the book, we've looked at a variety of important grammatical concepts that can facilitate the literacy development of early elementary school students, exploring the features, their impact on effective writing, published mentor texts that represent their uses, and instructional activities that can help students see these concepts as tools for effective writing. In this concluding chapter, we share five ideas that summarize important ideas from the book and will help you implement the approaches and activities in this book in your own classroom:

- Grammar instruction is most successful when it is viewed as a tool for effective writing.
- Mentor texts are an excellent way for students to understand the impact of grammatical concepts.
- Students learn from opportunities to apply their knowledge of grammatical concepts.
- Reflection is an important aspect of students' experiences learning about grammar.
- Strong grammar assessment aligns with and informs a toolkit-based instructional approach.

These insights represent key ideas in this book and provide manageable take-away insights to consider when you put the information described in this text into action. Let's now take a look at each one individually.

Closing Idea One: Grammar Instruction Is Most Successful When It Is Viewed as a Tool for Effective Writing

An essential aspect of the approach to grammar instruction that we discuss in this book is that grammatical concepts are tools for effective writing and that writers use them purposefully and strategically to make their writing as

DOI: 10.4324/9781003302209-13

strong as possible. All the grammatical concepts we describe—such as nouns, verbs, capitalization, commas, pronouns, and others—can all function as tools that writers have in their writing skillsets (or toolkits) that they can then use in intentional and meaningful ways to make their works as effective as possible. Because of this, when presenting grammatical concepts to students, we don't suggest focusing on students being able to immediately memorize the definitions and attributes of grammatical terms. Instead (as you've certainly noticed throughout the book!), we recommend using anchor charts to display fundamental ideas about grammatical concepts, such as information about the concept being discussed and examples of how it can look in action.

When we frame grammatical concepts as tools for effective writing in our teaching, we emphasize the purposeful uses of these concepts and help students not only use the strategies in their writing, but also understand the reasons why they would use them. By thinking about grammatical concepts as tools for effective writing and presenting them to students in those ways, we add to their abilities as writers and help them grow in their writing-related decision making. Grammar instruction that focuses on out-of-context worksheets and correcting mistakes has been found to be ineffective and disengaging (Wotjer, 1998); taking a toolkit-oriented approach can help students see grammatical concepts as meaningful concepts that they can purposefully use to make their writing strong and effective.

Closing Idea Two: Mentor Texts Are an Excellent Way for Students to Understand the Impact of Grammatical Concepts

When presenting grammatical concepts to students as tools for effective writing, we strongly recommend using mentor texts—examples from published texts that use the concepts effectively—in your instruction. Examining these published uses of grammatical concepts with your students has a number of benefits. One of these benefits is that it shows students that these concepts are used in authentic settings by published authors. This is significant because it communicates to students that grammar doesn't just exist in out-of-context examples and activities; instead, it's something that's used in real-world situations by authors and anyone else who wants to express an idea effectively and uses a grammatical tool to communicate that information. Another benefit of mentor text use is that it helps inspire conversations about the importance of grammatical concepts to effective writing. When we teachers show students examples of published grammar tools such as nouns, verbs, punctuation, capitalization, or any other concept, we can use those published examples to have conversations with students about why the use of that concept makes the piece effective.

All the mentor text examples we've presented in Chapters 1 through 10 of this book are strong models of the uses of their focal grammatical concepts and can form the basis of strong conversations with your students about the importance of these concepts to effective writing. As you share these examples (or others that represent the concepts well) with your students, we encourage you to talk with your students about why the grammatical concept on which you're focusing is important to the effectiveness of the text. For example, if you are discussing conjunctions with your students, you can use the following conjunction mentor text from the book *Hair Love* (Cherry & Harrison, 2019) described in Chapter 7: "My name is Zuri, and I have hair that has a mind of its own" (n.p.). In your discussion with your students of this exemplar, you can help them understand that this is an authentic example of the conjunction "and." After working with them to identify this conjunction use, you can talk with students about why the conjunction is important to the effectiveness of the passage in which it's used.

Closing Idea Three: Students Learn from Opportunities to Apply Their Knowledge of Grammatical Concepts

Another idea about effective grammar instruction that is essential to the approach and methods discussed in this book is our belief that students learn from opportunities to apply their knowledge of grammatical concepts. Once students have thought about grammatical concepts as tools for effective writing and looked closely at mentor texts containing those concepts, we believe that it's important for students to create their own examples of these concepts. When students apply their knowledge in this way, they take increased ownership of and responsibility for their learning. This opportunity for students to use the understanding they've developed about a grammatical concept to construct one of their own can deepen their learning experiences through meaningful application. As we've discussed in this book, there are a variety of specific ways students can create examples of concepts based on their individual levels of comfort and familiarity with writing: in addition to writing a sentence containing the focal concept, students can create examples in other ways, such as dictating text containing the concept to a teacher; drawing a picture that represents the concept and verbally explaining what's taking place, as well as well how the concept is relevant to it; and writing as much as they can of a sentence containing the concept and verbally sharing the rest.

While students create these examples, we recommend holding individualized conferences with them to monitor their progress and give them personalized support. During these conferences, we suggest asking students to identify the example of the concept they used and then to explain to you why they chose to use it. By answering these questions, students will show you how they incorporated the focal concept in their work and will convey their thought process for selecting the example of the concept that they did. Individualized writing conferences that focus on these topics will provide excellent opportunities for informal and formative assessment that gives students in-progress feedback on their work. For example, if you're conferring with a student about capitalization, you can ask them to show you capitalized words in their work and then to talk with you about why they capitalized those words. If students express any confusion with the content, such as uncertainty about why certain words should be capitalized, you can use this time to help them clarify any misunderstandings about the features and uses of the grammatical concept.

Closing Idea Four: Reflection Is an Important Aspect of Students' Experiences Learning About Grammar

To make grammar instruction as effective as possible, we recommend incorporating the idea of reflection in students' learning experiences. In the context of grammar instruction, this means building in time for students to think about why a particular grammatical concept is important to effective strong writing and supporting them as they process their ideas. We believe that when students reflect on the significance of grammatical concepts, they can deepen their understanding of those concepts as tools for effective writing. Developing this awareness of the role of grammatical concepts in strong writing is a key goal of the instructional approach we describe in this book. We don't want students to see the elements of grammar as terms to memorize and apply to out-of-context worksheets; instead, we want students to think about the benefits associated with grammatical concepts and the reasons writers use those concepts.

To engage students in this reflective work, we recommend asking students two questions related to each grammatical concept they study: 1) Why is this concept important to good writing? and 2) How would writing be different if this concept wasn't used? By considering these ideas, students will think about the role that the grammatical concept has on effective writing. Chapters 1 through 10 of this book all contain examples of these questions that align with the specific grammar tools discussed in those chapters. Regardless of the particular concept, the fundamental ideas behind these reflection questions remain the same: the questions are designed to help students consider each grammatical concept they study as a tool that makes writing stronger and that they can implement in their own works.

Closing Idea Five: Strong Grammar Assessment Aligns With and Informs a Toolkit-Based Instructional Approach

This final idea relates to effective and meaningful assessment of students' knowledge of grammatical concepts: we believe that effective grammar assessment provides students with opportunities to demonstrate their knowledge in authentic ways and reflect on the importance of the focal concept to the text they created. These opportunities for authentic application and reflection are aligned with the toolkit-oriented approach discussed in this book: instead of focusing on out-of-context assessments that are focused primarily on students' mistakes, they create ways for students to demonstrate their knowledge in ways that are authentic and are aligned with the instructional approach and corresponding practices discussed in this book. To do this with your students, we recommend using the graphic organizer template and corresponding rubric described in Chapter 11. By asking students to identify examples of the concepts they've studied, use them in sentences, draw pictures that correspond with those sentences, and reflect on the importance of the example they used, students will show their awareness of the features, usage, and importance of grammatical concepts.

When you assess students' work on this activity, you'll identify the accuracy with which they use the concept, their ability to incorporate it in a sentence, and the ideas they express when commenting on the importance of the concept to the sentence. It's especially important to note that these assessments will provide useful information that can inform your future instruction: as you evaluate how well students can create, use, and reflect on examples, you'll develop well-informed understandings of their awareness of the grammatical concepts you study with them. If there are any aspects of a student's work that can benefit from further instruction, you can address these ideas in follow-up mini-lessons and conversations. We believe that effective grammar assessment is not meant to penalize students for mistakes: it is instead a tool for students' authentic applications of knowledge that can be used to inform future instruction.

Final Points About the Early Elementary Grammar Toolkit

We wrote this book to provide early elementary school teachers with a mentor-text-based and student-centered resource to use when teaching grammar in effective and meaningful ways. The grammar toolkit approach we describe in this book frames grammar instruction in a new way for both teachers and students, empowering them to talk about grammatical concepts as tools that authors use strategically, with clear understandings of what each one does and how it plays an important role in effective writing. By presenting grammatical concepts to students as useful and meaningful tools, we move away from grammar instruction that focuses on correcting mistakes and toward an instructional approach that builds students' knowledge and insights. Through teaching and learning activities that incorporate mentor texts, student application, and reflection to help students understand what key grammatical concepts are and why they're important to effective writing, we help our students build lasting understandings of how and why writers use the elements of grammar to construct strong works that express their ideas effectively. By implementing this approach and the corresponding instructional activities in your classroom, you'll help your students learn and grow as writers. Please feel free to reach out to us if you have questions about your grammar instruction—we are passionate about using a toolkit-based approach to teach grammar and would be happy to help!

References

Arnold, T. (1997). *Parts*. Picture Puffin Books.

Barone, D. M., Xu, S. H., & Mallette, M. H. (2005). *Teaching early literacy: Development, assessment, and instruction* (2nd ed.). Guilford Press.

Blackburne, L., & Kuo, J. (2021). *I dream of Popo*. Roaring Brook Press.

Brown, P. (2010). *Children make terrible pets*. Little, Brown, and Company.

Bryant, J., & Morrison, F. (2020). *Above the rim: How Elgin Baylor changed basketball*. Harry N. Abrams.

Carle, E. (1969). *The very hungry caterpillar*. Penguin Books.

Charles, T., & Alcántara, J. (2021). *Freedom soup*. Candlewick.

Charles, T., & Collier, B. (2020). *All because you matter*. Orchard Books.

Cherry, M. A., & Harrison, V. (2019). *Hair love*. Kokila.

Coleman, D., Coleman, B., & Mello, B. (2020). *More than a princess*. Sydney & Coleman, LLC.

Cornwall, G. (2020). *Jabari jumps*. Candlewick Press.

de la Peña, M., & Robinson, C. (2016). *Last stop on market street*. Penguin Books.

de la Peña, M., & Robinson, C. (2018). *Carmela full of wishes*. G.P. Putnam's Sons Books for Young Readers.

de la Peña, M., & Robinson, C. (2021). *Milo imagines the world*. G.P. Putnam's Sons Books for Young Readers.

Dear Ranger Rick. (2017, June/July). *Ranger Rick*, 4.

Díaz, J., & Espinosa, L. (2018). *Islandborn*. Dial Books.

DiPucchio, K., & Figueroa, R. (2021). *Oona*. Katherine Tegan Books.

Duncan, A. F., & Bobo, K. A. (2022). *Opal Lee and what it means to be free*. Thomas Nelson.

Ferland, L., & Popova, Y. (2020). *We walk through the forest*. Lisa Ferland.

Flavell, J. H. (1979). Metacognition and cognitive monitoring. *American Psychologist, 34*, 906–911.

Garner, R. (1987). *Metacognition and reading comprehension*. Ablex.

Gibson, V. (2020, February 26). *Working toward culturally responsive assessment practices*. National Council of Teachers of English Blog. https://ncte.org/blog/2020/02/working-toward-culturally-responsive-assessment-practices

Gorman, A., & Long, L. (2021). *Change sings*. Viking Books for Young Readers.

Graham, S. (2019). Changing how writing is taught. *Review of Research in Education, 43*(1), 277–303.

Ho, J., & Ho, D. (2021). *Eyes that kiss in the corners*. HarperCollins.

Ho, J., & Ho, D. (2022). *Eyes that speak to the stars*. HarperCollins.

Joseph, J. (2020). *What will I be?* Independently Published.

Keats, E. J. (1962). *The snowy day*. Viking Books.

Khiani, D., & Lew-Vriethoff, J. (2021). *How to wear a sari*. Versify.

Killgallon, D., & Killgallon, J. (2010). *Grammar for college writing: A sentence composing approach*. Heinemann.

Lakshmi, P., & Martinez-Neal, J. (2021). *Tomatoes for Neela*. Viking Books for Young Readers.

Lanehart, S. L. (2002). *Sista, speak! Black women kinfolk talk about language and literacy*. University of Texas Press.

Lindstrom, C., & Goade, M. (2020). *We are water protectors*. Roaring Brook Press.

Maillard, K. N., & Martinez-Neal, J. (2019). *Fry bread*. Roaring Brook Press.

Mark, V., & Cloud, S. (2021). *Under the mango tree*. Sugar Apple Books.

McElmurry, J. (2006). *I'm not a baby!* Schwartz & Wade Books.

McKissack, P. C., & Isadora, R. (1986). *Flossie and the fox*. Dial Books for Young Readers.

National Council of Teachers of English. (2016). *NCTE professional knowledge for the teaching of writing*. https://ncte.org/statement/teaching-writing/

National Council of Teachers of English. (2018). *Statement on gender and language*. http://www2.ncte.org/statement/genderfairuseoflang/

Noor, N., & Ali, N. H. (2021). *Beautifully me*. Simon & Schuster Books for Young Readers.

Riley, C., & Kanavaliuk, A. (2020). *Not so different*. GreyNash.

Robb, L. (2001). *Grammar lessons and strategies that strengthen students' writing*. Scholastic.

Rose, T. (2022). *Dear reader*. Little Bee Books.

Ruday, S. (2013). *The common core grammar toolkit: Using mentor texts to teach the language standards in grades 3–5*. Routledge Eye on Education.

Ruday, S. (2017). *The common core grammar toolkit: Using mentor texts to teach the language standards in grades 9–12*. Routledge Eye on Education.

Ruday, S. (2020a). *The elementary school grammar toolkit: Using mentor texts to teach standards-based language and grammar in grades 3–5* (2nd ed.). Routledge Eye on Education.

Ruday, S. (2020b). *The middle school grammar toolkit: Using mentor texts to teach standards-based language and grammar in grades 6–8* (2nd ed.). Routledge Eye on Education.

Saeed, A., & Syed, A. (2019). *Bilal cooks daal*. Salaam Reads/Simon & Schuster Books for Young Readers.

Schardt, H. (2017, June/July). Cotton-top pop. *Ranger Rick*, 26–29.

Sendak, M. (1963). *Where the wild things are*. HarperCollins.

Stump Your Parents: Presidents Edition. (2021, February). *National Geographic Kids*, 28–29.

Tariq, A., & Lewis, S. (2021). *Fatima's great outdoors*. Kokila.

Thorpe, A. (2021). *The story of Jackie Robinson*. Rockridge Press.

Wang, A., & Chin, J. (2021). *Watercress*. Neal Porter Books.

Willems, M. (2010). *We are in a book*. Hyperion Books for Children.

Wilson, K., & Chapman, J. (2013). *Bear says thanks*. Scholastic.

Woodson, J., & López, R. (2022). *The year we learned to fly*. Nancy Paulsen Books.

Wotjer, S. (1998). Facilitating the use of description and grammar. In C. Weaver (Ed.), *Lessons to share on teaching grammar in context* (pp. 95–99). Boynton Cook.

Zhang, K., & Chua, C. (2019). *Amy Wu and the perfect bao*. Simon and Schuster Books for Young Readers.

Appendix A

Annotated Bibliography

This annotated bibliography contains the following information: 1) the titles, authors, and illustrators of the texts that we discuss in this book as exemplars of particular grammatical concepts; 2) a key grammatical concept found in each work; 3) an excerpt from that work, found earlier in this book, that demonstrates exactly how the author uses that grammar concept; and 4) information on the chapter of this book in which the concept is discussed (in case you want to refer back to the text for more information on a concept).

The annotated bibliography is designed to make this book as user-friendly as possible. It is organized alphabetically by author's last name and each entry includes important details designed to help you use mentor texts to teach these grammatical concepts.

Arnold, T. (1997). *Parts*. Picture Puffin Books.
Title: *Parts*
Author and Illustrator: Tedd Arnold
Grammatical Concept: End punctuation use
Excerpts that Demonstrate Concept:
"It was my stuffing coming out!" (n.p.)
"The glue that holds our parts together isn't holding me!!!" (n.p.)
Discussed in Chapter: 4

Blackburne, L., & Kuo, J. (2021). *I dream of Popo*. Roaring Brook Press.
Title: *I Dream of Popo*
Author: Livia Blackburne
Illustrator: Julia Kuo
Grammatical Concept: Effective verb use
Excerpt that Demonstrates Concept:
"I walk with Popo in the park, squeezing her finger in my chubby palm" (n.p.).
Discussed in Chapter: 2

Brown, P. (2010). *Children make terrible pets*. Little, Brown, and Company.
    Title: *Children Make Terrible Pets*
    Author and Illustrator: Peter Brown
    Grammatical Concept: Effective verb use
    Excerpt that Demonstrates Concept:
    "Lucy and Squeaker were inseparable" (n.p.).
    Discussed in Chapter: 2

Bryant, J., & Morrison, F. (2020). *Above the rim: How Elgin Baylor changed basketball*. Harry N. Abrams.
    Title: *Above the Rim: How Elgin Baylor Changed Basketball*
    Author: Jen Bryant
    Illustrator: Frank Morrison
    Grammatical Concept: Question word use
    Excerpt that Demonstrates Concept:
    " 'Where did he learn those moves?' the other players asked" (n.p.).
    Discussed in Chapter: 6

Carle, E. (1969). *The very hungry caterpillar*. Penguin Books.
    Author and Illustrator: Eric Carle
    Grammatical Concept: Capitalization
    Excerpt that Demonstrates Concept:
    "On Monday he ate through one apple" (n.p.).
    Discussed in Chapter: 5

Charles, T., & Alcántara, J. (2021). *Freedom soup*. Candlewick.
    Title: *Freedom Soup*
    Author: Tami Charles
    Illustrator: Jacqueline Alcántara
    Grammatical Concept: Effective noun use
    Excerpt that Demonstrates Concept:
    "The shake-shake of maracas vibrates down to my toes" (n.p.).
    Discussed in Chapter: 1

Charles, T., & Collier, B. (2020). *All because you matter*. Orchard Books.
    Title: *All Because You Matter*
    Author: Tami Charles
    Illustrator: Bryan Collier
    Grammatical Concept: Effective noun use
    Excerpt that Demonstrates Concept:

"Long before you took your place in this world, you were dreamed of, like a knapsack full of wishes, carried on the backs of your ancestors as they created empires, pyramids, legacies" (n.p.).
Discussed in Chapter: 1

Cherry, M. A., & Harrison, V. (2019). *Hair love*. Kokila.
Title: *Hair Love*
Author: Matthew A. Cherry
Illustrator: Vashti Harrison
Grammatical Concept: Conjunction use
Excerpt that Demonstrates Concept:
"My name is Zuri, and I have hair that has a mind of its own" (n.p.).
Discussed in Chapter: 7

Coleman, D., Coleman, B., & Mello, B. (2020). *More than a princess*. Sydney & Coleman, LLC.
Authors: Delanda Coleman & Beatrice Coleman
Illustrator: Beatriz Mello
Grammatical Concept: End punctuation use
Excerpt that Demonstrates Concept:
"What else would you like to explore, little one?" (n.p.)
Discussed in Chapter: 4

Cornwall, G. (2020). *Jabari jumps*. Candlewick Press.
Author and Illustrator: Gaia Cornwall
Grammatical Concept: Effective verb use
Excerpt that Demonstrates Concept:
"They spread their arms and bent their knees" (n.p).
Discussed in Chapter: 2

de la Peña, M., & Robinson, C. (2016). *Last stop on market street*. Penguin Books.
Title: *Last Stop on Market Street*
Author: Matt de la Peña
Illustrator: Christian Robinson
Grammatical Concept: Effective verb use
Excerpt that Demonstrates Concept:
"From the bus stop, he watched water pool on flower petals. Watched rain patter against the windshield of a nearby car" (n.p).
Discussed in Chapter: Introduction

de la Peña, M., & Robinson, C. (2018). *Carmela full of wishes*. G.P. Putnam's Sons Books for Young Readers.
   Title: *Carmela Full of Wishes*
   Author: Matt de la Peña
   Illustrator: Christian Robinson
   Grammatical Concept: Conjunction use
   Excerpt that Demonstrates Concept:
   "Carmela knew exactly what manure was, but she didn't want to think about that" (n.p.).
   ". . . imagining her dad getting his papers fixed so he could finally be home" (n.p.).
   Discussed in Chapter: 7

de la Peña, M., & Robinson, C. (2021). *Milo imagines the world*. G.P. Putnam's Sons Books for Young Readers.
   Title: *Milo Imagines the World*
   Author: Matt de la Peña
   Illustrator: Christian Robinson
   Grammatical Concept: Effective verb use
   Excerpt that Demonstrates Concept:
   ". . . Milo slips aboard" (n.p.).
   Discussed in Chapter: 2

Dear Ranger Rick. (2017, June/July). *Ranger Rick*, 4.
   Title: "Dear Ranger Rick."
   Author: Not identified
   Grammatical Concept: Comma use
   Excerpt that Demonstrates Concept:
   "Dear Ranger Rick," (p. 4).
   Discussed in Chapter: 9

Díaz, J., & Espinosa, L. (2018). *Islandborn*. Dial Books.
   Title: *Islandborn*
   Author: Junot Díaz
   Illustrator: Leo Espinosa
   Grammatical Concepts: Pronouns
   Excerpt that Demonstrates Concept:
   Lola, you see, loved to draw, but she left the island when she was just a baby so she didn't remember any of it" (n.p.).
   Discussed in Chapter: 10

DiPucchio, K., & Figueroa, R. (2021). *Oona*. Katherine Tegan Books.
    Title: *Oona*
    Author: Kelly DiPucchio
    Illustrator: Raissa Figueroa
    Grammatical Concepts: Pronouns
    Excerpt that Demonstrates Concept:
    "Oona was sweet . . . and a little bit salty, like the ocean where she lived.
    She was also brave and curious, like most treasure hunters" (n.p.).
    "'We did it!' Oona cheered, placing the crown on her best friend" (n.p.)
    Discussed in Chapter: 10

Duncan, A. F., & Bobo, K. A. (2022). *Opal Lee and what it means to be free*.
    Thomas Nelson.
    Title: *Opal Lee and What it Means to Be Free*
    Author: Alice Faye Duncan
    Illustrator: Keturah A. Bobo
    Grammatical Concept: Conjunction use
    Excerpt that Demonstrates Concept:
    "He danced a jig with cowboys playing fiddles, but they did not stop his
    flow" (n.p.).
    Discussed in Chapter: 7

Ferland, L., & Popova, Y. (2020). *We walk through the forest*. Lisa Ferland.
    Title: *We Walk Through the Forest*
    Author: Lisa Ferland
    Illustrator: Yana Popova
    Grammatical Concept: Question words
    Excerpts that Demonstrate Concept:
    "Birds sing, twigs snap, and leaves rustle. What's up ahead?" (n.p.)
    "We see—not a bear—but a silly old MOOSE!" (n.p.)
    "So, what gave you a scare?" (n.p.)
    Discussed in Chapter: 6

Gorman, A., & Long, L. (2021). *Change sings*. Viking Books for Young
    Readers.
    Title: *Change Sings*
    Author: Amanda Gorman
    Illustrator: Loren Long
    Grammatical Concepts: Plurals

Excerpt that Demonstrates Concept:
"I scream with the skies of red and blue streamers. I dream with the cries of tried and true dreamers" (n.p.).
Discussed in Chapter: 8

Ho, J., & Ho, D. (2021). *Eyes that kiss in the corners*. HarperCollins.
    Title: *Eyes That Kiss in the Corners*
    Author: Joanna Ho
    Illustrator: Dung Ho
    Grammatical Concept: Complete sentence
    Excerpt that Demonstrates Concept:
    "I have eyes that kiss in the corners and glow like warm tea" (n.p.).
    Discussed in Chapter: 3

Ho, J., & Ho, D. (2022). *Eyes that speak to the stars*. HarperCollins.
    Title: *Eyes That Speak to the Stars*
    Author: Joanna Ho
    Illustrator: Dung Ho
    Grammatical Concept: Conjunction use
    Excerpt that Demonstrates Concept:
    "Your eyes rise to the skies and speak to the stars" (n.p.).
    Discussed in Chapter: 7

Joseph, J. (2020). *What will I be?* Independently Published.
    Title: *What Will I Be?*
    Author and Illustrator: Jayla Joseph
    Grammatical Concept: Question words
    Excerpts that Demonstrate Concept:
    "What will I be?" (n.p)
    "How cool is that?" (n.p.)
    Discussed in Chapter: 6

Keats, E. J. (1962). *The snowy day*. Viking Books.
    Title: *The Snowy Day*
    Author and Illustrator: Ezra Jack Keats
    Grammatical Concept: Conjunction use
    Excerpt that Demonstrates Concept:
    "One winter morning Peter woke up and looked out the window" (n.p.).
    Discussed in Chapter: Introduction

Khiani, D., & Lew-Vriethoff, J. (2021). *How to wear a sari*. Versify.
Author: Darshana Khiani
Illustrator: Joanne Lew-Vriethoff
Grammatical Concept: End punctuation use
Excerpts that Demonstrate Concept:
"First, you need to find the perfect Sari" (n.p.).
"Gorgeous choice!" (n.p.).
Discussed in Chapter: 4

Lakshmi, P., & Martinez-Neal, J. (2021). *Tomatoes for Neela*. Viking Books for Young Readers.
Author: Padma Lakshmi
Illustrator: Juana Martinez-Neal
Grammatical Concepts: Plurals
Excerpt that Demonstrates Concept:
"Juicy ripe peaches, plump blueberries, golden corn topped with stringy silk so shiny, it looked like the hair on Neela's doll" (n.p).
Discussed in Chapter: 8

Lindstrom, C., & Goade, M. (2020). *We are water protectors*. Roaring Brook Press.
Title: *We are Water Protectors*
Author: Carole Lindstrom
Illustrator: Michaela Goade
Grammatical Concept: Complete sentence
Excerpt that Demonstrates Concept:
"We come from water" (n.p.).
Discussed in Chapter: 3

Maillard, K. N., & Martinez-Neal, J. (2019). *Fry bread*. Roaring Brook Press.
Title: *Fry Bread*
Author: Kevin Noble Maillard
Illustrator: Juanita Martinez-Neal
Grammatical Concept: Effective verb use
Excerpt that Demonstrates Concept:
"Hands mold the dough" (n.p).
Discussed in Chapter: 2

Mark, V., & Cloud, S. (2021). *Under the mango tree*. Sugar Apple Books.
  Title: *Under the Mango Tree*
  Author: Valdene Mark
  Illustrator: Sawyer Cloud
  Grammatical Concept: Effective noun use
  Excerpt that Demonstrates Concept:
  "Vee and Sanaa loved playing under the mango tree, its branches wide and tall, its bough heavy and strong" (n.p.).
  Discussed in Chapter: 1

McElmurry, J. (2006). *I'm not a baby!* Schwartz & Wade Books.
  Title: *I'm Not a Baby!*
  Author and Illustrator: Jill McElmurry
  Grammatical Concept: Question words
  Excerpts that Demonstrate Concept:
  "Where is our baby?" (n.p.)
  "Who ever said he was a baby?" (n.p.)
  Discussed in Chapter: 6

McKissack, P. C., & Isadora, R. (1986). *Flossie and the fox*. Dial Books for Young Readers.
  Author: Patricia C. McKissack
  Illustrator: Rachel Isadora
  Grammatical Concept: Capitalization
  Excerpt that Demonstrates Concept:
  " 'Here I am, Big Mama,' Flossie said after catching her breath. It was hot, hotter than a usual Tennessee August day" (n.p).
  Discussed in Chapter: 5

Noor, N., & Ali, N. H. (2021). *Beautifully me*. Simon & Schuster Books for Young Readers.
  Author: Nabela Noor
  Illustrator: Nabi H. Ali
  Grammatical Concept: End punctuation use
  Excerpts that Demonstrate Concept:
  "Yesterday, I woke up before the sun." (n.p.)
  "It was my first day of school!" (n.p.)
  "Why was Amma so sad?" (n.p.)
  Discussed in Chapter: 4

Riley, C., & Kanavaliuk, A. (2020). *Not so different*. GreyNash.
  Title: *Not So Different*
  Author: Cyana Riley
  Illustrator: Anastasia Kanavaliuk
  Grammatical Concept: Effective verb use
  Excerpt that Demonstrates Concept:
  "Everyone is different . . ." (n.p.).
  Discussed in Chapter: 2

Rose, T. (2022). *Dear reader*. Little Bee Books.
  Title: *Dear Reader*
  Author and Illustrator: Tiffany Rose
  Grammatical Concepts: Comma use
  Excerpts that Demonstrate Concept:
  "Dear Reader, do you see that little girl down there?" (n.p.).
  "Big books, small books, thin books, and tall books. Books about fish, alligators, science, and shells. Books of thrones, queens, friendship, and dreams" (n.p.).
  Discussed in Chapter: 9

Saeed, A., & Syed, A. (2019). *Bilal cooks daal*. Salaam Reads/Simon & Schuster Books for Young Readers.
  Title: *Bilal Cooks Daal*
  Author: Aisha Saeed
  Illustrator: Anoosha Syed
  Grammatical Concept: Complete sentence
  Excerpts that Demonstrate Concept:
  "They take off their shoes" (n.p.).
  "When Abu scoops out a cup of the bright yellow daal, it clatters in the bowl" (n.p.).
  "Bilal breathes in the scent of turmeric, chili, cumin" (n.p).
  Discussed in Chapter: 3

Schardt, H. (2017, June/July). Cotton-top pop. *Ranger Rick*, 26–29.
  Title: "Cotton-Top Pop"
  Author: Hannah Schardt
  Grammatical Concept: Comma use
  Excerpt that Demonstrates Concept:
  "The rest of their diet may not sound so scrumptious to you: insects, spiders, sap, and the occasional lizard" (p. 28).
  Discussed in Chapter: 9

Sendak, M. (1963). *Where the wild things are*. HarperCollins.
    Title: *Where the Wild Things Are*
    Author and Illustrator: Maurice Sendak
    Grammatical Concepts: Effective verb, adjective, and noun use
    Excerpt that Demonstrates Concept:
    " 'And now,' cried Max, 'let the wild rumpus start' " (n.p.).
    Discussed in Chapter: Introduction

Stump Your Parents: Presidents Edition. (2021, February). *National Geographic Kids*, 28–29.
    Title: "Stump Your Parents: Presidents Edition."
    Author: Not identified
    Grammatical Concept: Comma use
    Excerpt that Demonstrates Concept:
    "Which two presidents both died on July 4, 1826—the 50th anniversary of the Declaration of Independence?"
    Discussed in Chapter: 9

Tariq, A., & Lewis, S. (2021). *Fatima's great outdoors*. Kokila.
    Author: Ambreen Tariq
    Illustrator: Stevie Lewis
    Grammatical Concept: Capitalization
    Excerpt that Demonstrates Concept:
    "The trip felt like Fatima's reward after a long, hard week" (n.p.).
    Discussed in Chapter: 5

Thorpe, A. (2021). *The story of Jackie Robinson*. Rockridge Press.
    Title: *The Story of Jackie Robinson*
    Author: Andrea Thorpe
    Grammatical Concepts: Comma use
    Excerpt that Demonstrates Concept:
    "Jack Roosevelt Robinson was born on January 31, 1919" (n.p.).
    Discussed in Chapter: 9

Wang, A., & Chin, J. (2021). *Watercress*. Neal Porter Books.
    Title: *Watercress*
    Author: Andrea Wang
    Illustrator: Jason Chin
    Grammatical Concepts: Comma use
    Excerpt that Demonstrates Concept:

"... the red paint faded by years of glinting Ohio sun, pelting rain, and biting snow" (n.p.)
Discussed in Chapter: 9

Willems, M. (2010). *We are in a book*. Hyperion Books for Children.
   Title: *We Are in a Book*
   Author and Illustrator: Mo Willems
   Grammatical Concepts: Pronouns
   Excerpt that Demonstrates Concept:
   "We are in a book! We are being read!" (pp. 20–21).
   Discussed in Chapter: 10

Wilson, K., & Chapman, J. (2013). *Bear says thanks*. Scholastic.
   Title: *Bear Says Thanks*
   Author: Karma Wilson
   Illustrator: Jane Chapman
   Grammatical Concepts: Effective noun use
   Excerpt that Demonstrates Concept:
   No specific examples cited, but Kasey used this book to help her students understand nouns!
   Discussed in Chapter: 1

Woodson, J., & López, R. (2022). *The year we learned to fly*. Nancy Paulsen Books.
   Title: *The Year We Learned to Fly*
   Author: Jacqueline Woodson
   Illustrator: Rafael López
   Grammatical Concepts: Plurals
   Excerpt that Demonstrates Concept:
   "Lift your arms, close your eyes, take a deep breath, and believe in a thing" (n.p.).
   Discussed in Chapter: 8

Zhang, K., & Chua, C. (2019). *Amy Wu and the perfect bao*. Simon and Schuster Books for Young Readers.

Title: *Amy Wu and the Perfect Bao*
Author: Kat Zhang
Illustrator: Charlene Chua
Grammatical Concepts: Pronouns
Excerpt that Demonstrates Concept:
"Amy can do a lot of things. She can brush her teeth. She can tie her shoe" (n.p.)
Discussed in Chapter: 10

Appendix B

Reproducible Charts and Forms You Can Use in Your Classroom

This appendix features easily reproducible charts and forms that you can use in your classroom as you guide your early elementary students through discussions and activities related to how grammatical concepts are used as tools for effective writing. We encourage you to use these resources in tandem with the other materials provided in this book to maximize your experiences teaching your students about the tools of grammar and writing!

Example of Noun in the Mentor Text	Category to Which the Noun Belongs (Person, Place, Thing, or Idea)

Figure 1.3 Noun Category Graphic Organizer

Verb	What Makes It a Verb?	Why Might the Author Have Chosen to Use That Verb?

Figure 2.3 Verb Analysis Chart

Published Sentence	What Makes It a Complete Sentence	Why the Complete Sentence Is Important to the Story

Figure 3.2 Complete Sentence Discussion Graphic Organizer

Published Sentence	Why the Author Used the End Punctuation in the Sentence	How the Sentence Would Be Different if Other End Punctuation Was Used

Figure 4.2 End Punctuation Discussion Graphic Organizer

Capitalized Word	Reason It Is Capitalized

Figure 5.2 Capitalization Graphic Organizer

Question Word	Information Associated With It	Why We Think the Author Used This Question Word Here

Figure 6.3 Question Word Discussion Graphic Organizer

Sentence Containing a Conjunction	Conjunction Used in the Sentence	Benefits of Using This Conjunction

Figure 7.2 Conjunction Benefits Graphic Organizer

Plural Word From Published Text	How the Plural Form of the Word Is Created

Figure 8.2 Graphic Organizer: Plural Words and Constructions

Original Published Text	Text Without Plurals	Why the Plural Forms Are Important to the Original Text

Figure 8.3 Plural Reflection Graphic Organizer

Original Published Sentence	Published Sentence Without Commas	Reflection: Why Is Using Commas Important to This Example?	Reflection: How Is the Example Different When We Take the Commas Away?

Figure 9.2 Graphic Organizer for Published Comma Examples and Student Reflections

Original Published Sentence	Key Pronouns Used in the Sentence	Sentence Without Those Pronouns	Why Those Pronouns Are Important to the Passage

Figure 10.3 Graphic Organizer: Published Pronoun Analysis

Concept:	Example:

Use the example in a sentence:

Draw a picture of what's happening in the sentence:

Why the example of the concept is important to the sentence:

Figure 11.1 Student Assessment Graphic Organizer Template

(This is in a separate document called Student Assessment Graphic Organizer Template. An image of the graphic organizer template follows as well.)

Component and Explanation	Score (Out of four points for each category)	Comments
Accuracy of example Is the example of the grammatical concept accurate? Does it show an understanding of what the concept is?	/4	
Use in a sentence Is the concept used accurately and effectively in a sentence? Does the use of the concept in a sentence show an understanding of the concept?	/4	
Explanation of the importance of the concept to the sentence Is the explanation of the importance to the concept detailed and informative? Does it demonstrate a strong understanding of the concept?	/4	

Total score: /12
Concluding comments:

Figure 11.2 Sample Assessment Evaluation Rubric